太上感应篇，了凡四训

Heavenly Induction, Liaofan's Four Lessons

Translated by Donia Davia Zhang

Chinese Culture Publishing

While every precaution has been taken in the preparation of this book, the publisher assumes no responsibility for errors or omissions, or for damages resulting from the use of the information contained herein.

HEAVENLY INDUCTION, LIAOFAN'S FOUR LESSONS

First edition. August 6, 2025.

English Translation Copyright © 2025 Donia Davia Zhang.

ISBN: 978-1-7782861-4-8

Translated by Donia Davia Zhang.

Contents

Part 1: 太上感应篇   1
Heavenly Induction

Part 2: 了凡四训   28
Liaofan's Four Lessons

Lesson 1: 立命之学   29
Learning to Establish Destiny

Lesson 2: 改过之法   47
Ways to Correct Oneself

Lesson 3: 积善之方   57
Ways to Accumulate Kindness

Lesson 4: 谦德之效   90
Effects of Modesty and Virtue

Part 1: Heavenly Induction

Introduction

Taishang Ganying Pian, translated into English as *Heavenly Induction*, is a Daoist scripture from the Song dynasty (960–1279) to persuade people to obey moral norms, always stop evil, cultivate kindness, and benefit oneself and others. The chapter places special emphasis on the "Law of Responsibility," which was systematically put forward in the Daoist classic *Taiping Jing* (*Scripture on Great Peace*) in the Eastern Han dynasty (25–220). The law of responsibility, according to Huanglao (early 2nd century BCE), is that if people had done evil, their offspring would suffer misfortune, and if people had done good, their offspring would be blessed. It suggests that ancestral behavior had a butterfly effect on their descendants. The premise is that people first bear their own good or evil retribution during their lifetime, then to their descendants. A family that had accumulated kindness would bring more celebrations, and a family that had accumulated evil would bring more calamities. *Taishang Ganying Pian* is an important Daoist text reputed as the "first Chinese book on kindness since ancient times." From imperial Chinese court to common households, many people had disseminated it that reached a peak in the Ming (1368–1644) and Qing (1616–1911) dynasties. Many of the contents still have significant social implications today.

太上感应篇
Heavenly Induction

太上曰：

Tài shàng yuē:

祸福无门，惟人自召。

Huò fú wú mén, wéi rén zì zhào.

善恶之报，如影随形。

Shàn è zhī bào, rú yǐng suí xíng.

Taishang Laojun (Supreme One) said:

Adverse or good fortunes do not enter through a gate,

They are caused by the behaviors of people themselves.

What goes around comes around,

Just like the shadow follows the figure closely.

天地有司过之神，

Tiān dì yǒu sī guò zhī shén,

依人所犯轻重，以夺人算。

Yī rén suǒ fàn qīng zhòng, yǐ duó rén suàn.

算减则贫耗，多逢忧患，

Suàn jiǎn zé pín hào, duō féng yōu huàn,

人皆恶之，刑祸随之，

Rén jiē wù zhī, xíng huò suí zhī,

吉庆避之，恶星灾之，算尽则死。

Jí qìng bì zhī, è xīng zāi zhī, suàn jìn zé sǐ.

Between heaven and earth,
There are gods who manage faults,
According to the severity of the faults,
Their lifespan will be reduced.
Not only their lifespan reduced,
They will also suffer from poverty or loss,
Tribulations will come successively,
Everyone will hate them,
Punishments and calamities will follow them,
Auspiciousness and celebrations will avoid them,
Demons will bring disasters to them,
When their time is up, death will follow them.

又有三台北斗神君，在人头上，

Yòu yǒu sān tái běi dǒu shén jūn, zài rén tóu shàng,

录人罪恶，夺其纪算。

Lù rén zuì è, duó qí jì suàn.

又有三尸神，在人身中，

Yòu yǒu sān shī shén, zài rén shēn zhōng,

每到庚申日，辄上诣天曹，言人罪过。

Měi dào gēng shēn rì, zhé shàng yì tiān cáo, yán rén zuì guò.

There are three gods above people's heads,
They record people's faults and reduce their lifespans.
There are also three demons in the human body:
The upper demon Peng Ju is residing in the brain,
The middle demon Peng Zhi is living in the chest,

The lower demon Peng Jiao is staying in the abdomen.

They go to the heavenly office on the Gengshen Day:

Once every 60 days, to report people's crimes.

月晦之日，灶神亦然。

Yuè huì zhī rì, zào shén yì rán.

凡人有过，大则夺纪，小则夺算。

Fán rén yǒu guò, dà zé duó jì, xiǎo zé duó suàn.

其过大小，有数百事，

Qí guò dà xiǎo, yǒu shù bǎi shì,

欲求长生者，先须避之。

Yù qiú cháng shēng zhě, xiān xū bì zhī.

On the last day of each lunar month,

The Stove God will also report the family's faults.

If the fault is big, lifespan will be cut by 12 years.

If the fault is small, lifespan will be cut by 100 days.

There are more than 100 kinds of faults, big or small.

Those who want to prolong their lives,

They must first avoid big or small faults.

是道则进，非道则退。

Shì dào zé jìn, fēi dào zé tuì.

不履邪径，不欺暗室。

Bù lǚ xié jìng, bù qī àn shì.

If it is in line with the Dao, then proceed.

If it is not in line with the Dao, then retreat.

Do not take the evil path,

Do not lie to yourself in the dark.

积德累功，慈心于物。

Jī dé lěi gōng, cí xīn yú wù.

忠孝友悌，正己化人。

Zhōng xiào yǒu tì, zhèng jǐ huà rén.

矜孤恤寡，敬老怀幼。

Jīn gū xù guǎ, jìng lǎo huái yòu.

Accumulate virtue and merit, be kind to all things.

Be loyal to the country, be filial to your parents,

And love your siblings.

Correct yourself first and then teach others.

Sympathize with the loners and the helpless.

Respect the elderly and love others' children.

昆虫草木，犹不可伤。

Kūn chóng cǎo mù, yóu bù kě shāng.

宜悯人之凶，乐人之善，

Yí mǐn rén zhī xiōng, lè rén zhī shàn,

济人之急，救人之危。

Jì rén zhī jí, jiù rén zhī wēi.

Do not harm insects or plants.
Pity those who are in trouble,
Be happy for those who succeed.
Help those who are in need,
Rescue those who are in danger.

见人之得，如己之得。

Jiàn rén zhī dé, rú jǐ zhī dé.

见人之失，如己之失。

Jiàn rén zhī shī, rú jǐ zhī shī.

不彰人短，不衒己长。

Bù zhāng rén duǎn, bú xuàn jǐ cháng.

遏恶扬善，推多取少。

È è yáng shàn, tuī duō qǔ shǎo.

See the gains of others as your own.
Feel the losses of others as your own.
Do not publicize others' shortcomings,
Do not boast about your advantages.
Stop the evil and promote the good,
Give more and take less for yourself.

受辱不怨，受宠若惊。

Shòu rǔ bú yuàn, shòu chǒng ruò jīng.

施恩不求报，与人不追悔。

Shī ēn bù qiú bào, yǔ rén bù zhuī huǐ.

Do not resent when being insulted,
Be afraid of being favored.
Give without expecting anything in return,
Give what is in the heart without regret.

所谓善人，人皆敬之，
Suǒ wèi shàn rén, rén jiē jìng zhī,
天道佑之，福禄随之，
Tiān dào yòu zhī, fú lù suí zhī,
众邪远之，神灵卫之，
Zhòng xié yuǎn zhī, shén líng wèi zhī,
所作必成，神仙可冀。
Suǒ zuò bì chéng, shén xiān kě jì.

The so-called kind people, everyone respects them,
The Dao bless them, good fortunes follow them,
The demons distance them, the gods protect them,
They succeed in what they do and become immortals.

欲求天仙者，当立一千三百善，
Yù qiú tiān xiān zhě, dāng lì yì qiān sān bǎi shàn,
欲求地仙者，当立三百善。
Yù qiú dì xiān zhě, dāng lì sān bǎi shàn.

Those who wish to attain celestial immortality,
They should accumulate 1,300 good deeds.
Those who wish to obtain telestial immortality,
They should accumulate 300 good deeds.

苟或非义而动，背理而行。
Gǒu huò fēi yì ér dòng, bèi lǐ ér xíng.
以恶为能，忍作残害。
Yǐ è wéi néng, rěn zuò cán hài.
阴贼良善，暗侮君亲。
Yīn zéi liáng shàn, àn wǔ jūn qīn.
慢其先生，叛其所事。
Màn qí xiān shēng, pàn qí suǒ shì.

If those think about unrighteous things,
They could act irrationally.
They could have the power of evil, and the heart to kill.
They could secretly harm good people,
Deceive officials and their parents.
They could be rude to their teachers,
And irresponsible for their actions.

诳诸无识，谤诸同学。
Kuáng zhū wú shí, bàng zhū tóng xué.
虚诬诈伪，攻讦宗亲。
Xū wū zhà wěi, gōng jié zōng qīn.

刚强不仁，狠戾自用。

Gāng qiáng bù rén, hěn lì zì yòng.

是非不当，向背乖宜。

Shì fēi bú dàng, xiàng bèi guāi yí.

虐下取功，谄上希旨。

Nüè xià qǔ gōng, chǎn shàng xī zhǐ.

受恩不感，念怨不休。

Shòu ēn bù gǎn, niàn yuàn bù xiū.

Do not deceive the ignorant or slander classmates.

Do not wrong the good or find fault in the clan.

Do not be unbenevolent or cruel.

Do not take right as wrong or wrong as right.

Do not get close to the evil or distance the good.

Do not use deceitful means to flatter,

Or cater for the superiors' wishes.

Do not receive favors without showing gratitude,

Or hold resentment endlessly.

轻蔑天民，扰乱国政。

Qīng miè tiān mín, rǎo luàn guó zhèng.

赏及非义，刑及无辜。

Shǎng jí fēi yì, xíng jí wú gū.

杀人取财，倾人取位。

Shā rén qǔ cái, qīng rén qǔ wèi.

诛降戮服，贬正排贤。

Zhū jiàng lù fú, biǎn zhèng pái xián.

凌孤逼寡，弃法受赂。

Líng gū bī guǎ, qì fǎ shòu lù.

以直为曲，以曲为直。

Yǐ zhí wéi qū, yǐ qū wéi zhí.

Do not despise commoners or disturb the state affairs.
Do not reward the unrighteous or punish the innocent.
Do not murder for money or use tricks to get a position.
Do not kill surrenders, expel the just, or reject the wise.
Do not bully the orphans or coerce the widows.
Do not abandon the laws or give or accept bribes.
Do not take straight as curved or curved as straight.

入轻为重，见杀加怒。

Rù qīng wéi zhòng, jiàn shā jiā nù.

知过不改，知善不为。

Zhī guò bù gǎi, zhī shàn bù wéi.

自罪引他，壅塞方术。

Zì zuì yǐn tā, yōng sè fāng shù.

讪谤圣贤，侵凌道德。

Shàn bàng shèng xián, qīn líng dào dé.

射飞逐走，发蛰惊栖，

Shè fēi zhú zǒu, fā zhé jīng qī,

填穴覆巢，伤胎破卵。

Tián xué fù cháo, shāng tāi pò luǎn.

Do not punish misdemeanors heavily,

Or get angry at those on the verge of death.

Do not keep making mistakes,

Or not doing good deeds.

Do not involve others intentionally in your misconduct,

Or keep healthy methods secretly.

Do not ridicule or slander sages,

Or persecute the virtuous.

Do not shoot flying birds, chase beasts,

Dig insects or frighten passerines.

Do not fill caves to prevent insects, birds,

Or beasts from living inside.

Do not harm gravid animals or break their eggs.

愿人有失，毁人成功。

Yuàn rén yǒu shī, huǐ rén chéng gōng.

危人自安，减人自益。

Wēi rén zì ān, jiǎn rén zì yì.

以恶易好，以私废公。

Yǐ è yì hǎo, yǐ sī fèi gōng.

窃人之能，蔽人之善。

Qiè rén zhī néng, bì rén zhī shàn.

Do not wish others to fail or destroy their success.

Do not put others in danger to obtain your security.

Do not reduce others' benefits to increase your profits.

Do not use bad stuff to exchange for others' good stuff.

Do not impede public welfare for your personal gains.

Do not steal others' work to conceal their merits.

形人之丑，讦人之私。

Xíng rén zhī chǒu, jié rén zhī sī.

耗人货财，离人骨肉。

Hào rén huò cái, lí rén gǔ ròu.

侵人所爱，助人为非。

Qīn rén suǒ ài, zhù rén wéi fēi.

逞志作威，辱人求胜。

Chěng zhì zuò wēi, rǔ rén qiú shèng.

败人苗稼，破人婚姻。

Bài rén miáo jià, pò rén hūn yīn.

Do not spread others' scandals or expose their secrets.

Do not ruin others' assets or damage their properties.

Do not cause others' separation from their loved ones.

Do not loot what others love or help them to do evil.

Do not indulge your own will, or insult others to win.

Do not damage others' crops or break their marriages.

苟富而骄，苟免无耻。

Gǒu fù ér jiāo, gǒu miǎn wú chǐ.

认恩推过，嫁祸卖恶。

Rèn ēn tuī guò, jià huò mài è.

沽买虚誉，包贮险心。

Gū mǎi xū yù, bāo zhù xiǎn xīn.

挫人所长，护己所短。

Cuò rén suǒ cháng, hù jǐ suǒ duǎn.

乘威迫胁，纵暴杀伤。

Chéng wēi pò xié, zòng bào shā shāng.

Do not be arrogant after getting rich,

Or repeat the same mistake shamelessly.

Do not take credit for others' work,

Or blame others for your faults.

Do not transfer your faults to others.

Do not buy or sell fake names,

Or contain a sinister heart.

Do not prevent others from growing,

Or conceal your shortcomings.

Do not rely on power to coerce others,

Or indulge in violence and killing.

无故剪裁，非礼烹宰。

Wú gù jiǎn cái, fēi lǐ pēng zǎi.

散弃五谷，劳扰众生。

Sàn qì wǔ gǔ, láo rǎo zhòng shēng.

破人之家，取其财宝。

Pò rén zhī jiā, qǔ qí cái bǎo.

决水放火，以害民居。

Jué shuǐ fàng huǒ, yǐ hài mín jū.

紊乱规模，以败人功。

Wěn luàn guī mó, yǐ bài rén gōng.

损人器物，以穷人用。

Sǔn rén qì wù, yǐ qióng rén yòng.

Do not tailor your clothes just for fashion,

Or kill and cook animals for food.

Do not waste grains or exhaust your laborers.

Do not break others to obtain their wealth.

Do not destroy dikes or set fires to harm people.

Do not ruin others' business to defeat their efforts.

Do not damage others' items to make them useless.

见他荣贵，愿他流贬。

Jiàn tā róng guì, yuàn tā liú biǎn.

见他富有，愿他破散。

Jiàn tā fù yǒu, yuàn tā pò sàn.

见他色美，起心私之。

Jiàn tā sè měi, qǐ xīn sī zhī.

负他货财，愿他身死。

Fù tā huò cái, yuàn tā shēn sǐ.

Do not wish others to be demoted,

After seeing their splendor.

Do not wish others to lose,

After seeing their family's wealth.

Do not raise a lustful heart,

After seeing others' wives' beauty.

Do not wish others to die,

If you owe the debt and must repay.

干求不遂，便生咒恨。

Gān qiú bù suí, biàn shēng zhòu hèn.

见他失便，便说他过。

Jiàn tā shī biàn, biàn shuō tā guò.

见他体相不具而笑之。

Jiàn tā tǐ xiàng bú jù ér xiào zhī.

见他才能可称而抑之。

Jiàn tā cái néng kě chēng ér yì zhī.

Do not curse others if you cannot obtain what you want.

Do not discuss others' faults after seeing their failures.

Do not laugh at others after seeing their ugly appearance.

Do not belittle but praise others after seeing their talents.

埋蛊厌人，用药杀树。

Mái gǔ yàn rén, yòng yào shā shù.

恚怒师傅，抵触父兄。

Huì nù shī fù, dǐ chù fù xiōng.

强取强求，好侵好夺。

Qiǎng qǔ qiǎng qiú, hào qīn hào duó.

掳掠致富，巧诈求迁。

Lǔ lüè zhì fù, qiǎo zhà qiú qiān.

赏罚不平，逸乐过节。

Shǎng fá bù píng, yì lè guò jié.

Do not poison people secretly,

Or kill vegetation with toxins.

Do not be rude to teachers,

Or conflict with family members.

Do not coerce to gain,

Or use cunning tactics to obtain things.

Do not kidnap, rob, steal,

Or deceive to get rich and promoted.

Do not reward or punish others unfairly,

Or indulge without restraint.

苛虐其下，恐吓于他。

Kē nüè qí xià, kǒng hè yú tā.

怨天尤人，诃风骂雨。

Yuàn tiān yóu rén, hē fēng mà yǔ.

斗合争讼，妄逐朋党。

Dòu hé zhēng sòng, wàng zhú péng dǎng.

用妻妾语，违父母训。

Yòng qī qiè yǔ, wéi fù mǔ xùn.

得新忘故，口是心非。

Dé xīn wàng gù, kǒu shì xīn fēi.

Do not abuse or scare the subordinates and servants.
Do not complain or scold if things go against your will.
Do not cause conflict in groups to make profits from it.
Do not join illegal associations and follow their voices.
Do not take wife's words to violate parents' teachings.
Do not favor the new but forget the old or be deceitful.

贪冒于财，欺罔其上。

Tān mào yú cái, qī wǎng qí shàng.

造作恶语，谗毁平人。

Zào zuò è yǔ, chán huǐ píng rén.

毁人称直，骂神称正。

Huǐ rén chēng zhí, mà shén chēng zhèng.

弃顺效逆，背亲向疏。

Qì shùn xiào nì, bèi qīn xiàng shū.

Do not embezzle money and deceive your boss.
Do not fabricate bad stories and spread rumors.
Do not ruin others' names and call this honesty.
Do not condemn the gods and call this integrity.
Do not abandon the natural law or go against it.
Do not ignore your relatives but favor strangers.

指天地以证鄙怀，

Zhǐ tiān dì yǐ zhèng bǐ huái,

引神明而鑑猥事。

Yǐn shén míng ér jiàn wěi shì.

施与后悔，假借不还。

Shī yǔ hòu huǐ, jiǎ jiè bù huán.

分外营求，力上施设。

Fèn wài yíng qiú, lì shàng shī shè.

Do not ask heaven and earth
to witness your despicable intentions.
Do not invite the gods to observe
and inspect your obscene actions.
Do not regret what you've given
or pretend to borrow without return.
Do not seek what is not yours
or focus your efforts on showy facilities.

淫欲过度，心毒貌慈。

Yín yù guò dù, xīn dú mào cí.

秽食餧人，左道惑众。

Huì shí wèi rén, zuǒ dào huò zhòng.

短尺狭度，轻秤小升。

Duǎn chǐ xiá dù, qīng chèng xiǎo shēng.

以伪杂真，採取奸利。

Yǐ wěi zá zhēn, cǎi qǔ jiān lì.

压良为贱，谩蓦愚人。

Yā liáng wéi jiàn, màn mò yú rén.

Do not have excessive sexual behavior,
Or a vicious heart but a kind appearance.
Do not give foul food to people to eat,
Or use sorcery to confuse the commoners.
Do not use unequal weight or false scale
to gain illegal returns.
Do not mix fake products with real ones
to take treacherous profits.
Do not coerce the innocent to act lowly,
Or deceive the unintelligent to believe.

贪婪无厌，咒诅求直。

Tān lán wú yàn, zhòu zǔ qiú zhí.

嗜酒悖乱，骨肉忿争。

Shì jiǔ bèi luàn, gǔ ròu fèn zhēng.

男不忠良，女不柔顺。

Nán bù zhōng liáng, nǚ bù róu shùn.

不和其室，不敬其夫。

Bù hé qí shì, bú jìng qí fū.

每好矜夸，常行妒忌。

Měi hào jīn kuā, cháng xíng dù jì.

Do not be greedy or dissatisfied

or curse yourself to prove righteousness.

Do not be addicted to alcohol or act badly,

or cause conflicts in the family.

Do not be unfaithful to your wife as a man

or be ungentle as a woman.

Do not mistreat your wife or disrespect your husband

to cause disharmony.

Do not boast or arouse jealousy and suspicion

between husband and wife.

无行于妻子，失礼于舅姑。

Wú xíng yú qī zǐ, shī lǐ yú jiù gū.

轻慢先灵，违逆上命。

Qīng màn xiān líng, wéi nì shàng mìng.

作为无益，怀挟外心。

Zuò wéi wú yì, huái jiá wài xīn.

自咒咒他，偏憎偏爱。

Zì zhòu zhòu tā, piān zēng piān ài.

Do not speak bad words or do bad deeds

to your wife and children.

Do not have improper etiquette

when serving the in-laws.

Do not violate rituals of sacrifice for ancestors,

or the orders of superiors.

Do not do selfish things unconducive

to individual, society, or country.

Do not have resentment in your heart,

or curse and treat others unfairly.

Do not favor those you love,

or disfavor those you hate.

越井越灶，跳食跳人。

Yuè jǐng yuè zào, tiào shí tiào rén.

损子堕胎，行多隐僻。

Sǔn zǐ duò tāi, xíng duō yǐn pì.

晦腊歌舞，朔旦号怒。

Huì là gē wǔ, shuò dàn hào nù.

Do not cross wells or stoves,

or jump over food or people.

Do not have an abortion,

or be unable to do things openly.

Do not sing or dance at year-end

to miss important events.

Do not get angry or cry

on the first day of the lunar month.

对北涕唾及溺，对灶吟咏及哭。

Duì běi tì tuò jí nì, duì zào yín yǒng jí kū.

又以灶火烧香，秽柴作食。

Yòu yǐ zào huǒ shāo xiāng, huì chái zuò shí.

夜起裸露，八节行刑。

Yè qǐ luǒ lù, bā jié xíng xíng.

[八节：立春、春分、立夏、夏至、

立秋、秋分、立冬、冬至]

[Bā jié: Lì chūn, chūn fēn, lì xià, xià zhì,

Lì qiū, qiū fēn, lì dōng, dōng zhì]

Do not face north to blow your nose, spit, or urinate,

Or face the stove to sing or cry.

Do not use cooking fire to light incense,

Or use filthy and unclean wood to cook food.

Do not wake up naked at night,

Or execute a criminal on the Eight Solar Terms.

[The Eight Solar Terms include:

Start of Spring, Spring Equinox,
Start of Summer, Summer Solstice,
Start of Autumn, Autumn Equinox,
Start of Winter, Winter Solstice]

唾流星，指虹霓。
Tuò liú xīng, zhǐ hóng ní.
辄指三光，久视日月。
Zhé zhǐ sān guāng, jiǔ shì rì yuè.
春月燎猎，对北恶骂。
Chūn yuè liáo liè, duì běi è mà.
无故杀龟打蛇。
Wú gù shā guī dǎ shé.

Do not spit at meteors or point at a rainbow.
Do not point at the sun, the moon, the stars.
Do not stare at the sun or the moon for long.
Do not burn forests for hunting in the spring.
Do not say bad words toward the north.
Do not kill turtles or snakes for no reason.

如是等罪，司命随其轻重，
Rú shì děng zuì, sī mìng suí qí qīng zhòng,
夺其纪算，算尽则死。
Duó qí jì suàn, suàn jìn zé sǐ.
死有余责，乃殃及子孙。
Sǐ yǒu yú zé, nǎi yāng jí zǐ sūn.

又诸横取人财者，

Yòu zhū héng qǔ rén cái zhě,

乃计其妻子家口以当之，渐至死丧。

Nǎi jì qí qī zǐ jiā kǒu yǐ dāng zhī, jiàn zhì sǐ sàng.

For the faults listed above,

The God of Command will punish the person,

According to the severeness of the fault,

The severest is death penalty.

If death would not be a sufficient punishment,

Their descendants will bear the outcomes of the disaster.

If a man coerces to obtain others' possessions,

The God of Command will guess the assets of his family,

So that they will suffer equal retribution and perish.

若不死丧，则有水火、盗贼、遗亡器物、

Ruò bù sǐ sàng, zé yǒu shuǐ huǒ, dào zéi, yí wáng qì wù,

疾病、口舌诸事，以当妄取之直。

Jí bìng, kǒu shé zhū shì, yǐ dāng wàng qǔ zhī zhí.

又枉杀人者，是易刀兵而相杀也。

Yòu wǎng shā rén zhě, shì yì dāo bīng ér xiāng shā yě.

取非义之财者，譬如漏脯救饥，

Qǔ fēi yì zhī cái zhě, pì rú lòu fǔ jiù jī,

鸩酒止渴，非不暂饱，死亦及之。

Zhèn jiǔ zhǐ kě, fēi bú zàn bǎo, sǐ yì jí zhī.

If they are fortunate enough to survive from death,
There will be floods, fires, thefts, lost tools,
Illnesses, quarrels, and so on.
The severity of retribution is equal to the
Values of others' assets they have taken.
And those who kill people unfairly,
It is like killing each other with swords.
Those who seize illegal profits,
It is like eating poisonous meat to quell hunger,
Or drinking toxic wine to quench thirst.
Which will not only fail to ease their hunger,
But it will also lead to their demise.

夫心起于善，善虽未为，而吉神已随之。
Fū xīn qǐ yú shàn, shàn suī wèi wéi, ér jí shén yǐ suí zhī.
或心起于恶，恶虽未为，而凶神已随之。
Huò xīn qǐ yú è, è suī wèi wéi, ér xiōng shén yǐ suí zhī.

If they think kind thoughts in their minds,
Although they have not done the good deeds,
The divine is already following them.
If they think evil thoughts in their minds,
Even though they have not done the bad deeds,
The demon is already following them.

其有曾行恶事，后自改悔。

Qí yǒu céng xíng è shì, hòu zì gǎi huǐ.

诸恶莫作，众善奉行。

Zhū è mò zuò, zhòng shàn fèng xíng.

久久必获吉庆，

Jiǔ jiǔ bì huò jí qìng,

所谓转祸为福也。

Suǒ wèi zhuǎn huò wéi fú yě.

Some people had done bad deeds,
But later they repented and changed.
Stop doing any type of bad deeds,
Start doing all kinds of good deeds.
Over time, one will gain auspiciousness
And have celebrations.
This is called turning misfortune into good fortune.

故吉人语善、视善、行善，

Gù jí rén yǔ shàn, shì shàn, xíng shàn,

一日有三善，三年天必降之福。

Yī rì yǒu sān shàn, sān nián tiān bì jiàng zhī fú.

凶人语恶、视恶、行恶，

Xiōng rén yǔ è, shì è, xíng è,

一日有三恶，三年天必降之祸。

Yī rì yǒu sān è, sān nián tiān bì jiàng zhī huò.

胡不勉而行之？

Hú bù miǎn ér xíng zhī?

Thus, fortunate people speak good words,
Watch good things and do good deeds.
If they do three good deeds every day,
When accumulating these for three years,
Heaven will send them good fortunes.
Unfortunate people speak evil words,
Watch evil things and do evil deeds.
If they do three evil deeds every day,
When accumulating these for three years,
Heaven will bring them misfortunes.
So, why not diligently do good and avoid evil?

Part 2: Liaofan's Four Lessons

Introduction

During China's Ming dynasty (1368–1644), Yuan Liaofan (1533–1606) wrote *Liaofan's Four Lessons* (*Liaofan Si Xun*), with the hope of teaching his son, Yuan Tianqi, to understand true destiny and practice good deeds: "Do good even if it is a small good deed," and "do not do evil even if it is a small evil act." In this way, one can change their destiny. The sayings "break evil and cultivate good," "disasters will go, and blessings will come," are true testimonies of transforming one's destiny. Through his life experience, Yuan Liaofan provided living proof of the benefits of practicing good deeds and cultivating virtue and humility. The title, *Liaofan's Four Lessons,* embodies his teaching. "Liaofan" suggests that it is inadequate to be ordinary, strive to be outstanding. There are four lessons (chapters) in the book. The first lesson shows how to establish a destiny. The second lesson suggests ways to correct oneself. The third lesson reveals the ways to accumulate kindness. And the fourth lesson discloses the effects of modesty and virtue.

了凡四训·第一章·立命之学

Liaofan's Four Lessons

Lesson 1: Learning to Establish Destiny

余童年丧父，老母命弃举业学医，谓可以养生，可以济人，且习一艺以成名，尔父夙心也。后余在慈云寺，遇一老者，修髯伟貌，飘飘若仙，余敬礼之。语余曰："子仕路中人也，明年即进学，何不读书？"

My father passed away when I was a child, my mother asked me to give up scholarly study and not to take the Imperial Examination, but to learn medicine instead, as she said learning medicine could make money to support the family while helping others. If I could master medical skills, I could become a famous doctor. This was also my father's wish. Later, at the Ciyun (lit. "Merciful Cloud") Temple, I met an old man who had an extraordinary appearance and a long beard, looking like an immortal. I saluted him. The old man said to me: "You will be in officialdom. You should take the exam and enter the academy next year. Why don't you study?"

余告以故，并叩老者姓氏里居。曰："吾姓孔，云南人也。得邵子皇极数正传，数该传汝。"余引之归，告母。母曰："善待之。"试其数，纤悉皆验。

I explained to the old man why my mother asked me to give up scholarly study but to learn medicine. I then inquired about his name and hometown. The old man said: "My family name is Kong, and I am from Yunnan. I received authentic tradition of calculating the Destiny Number from Shao Kangjie [1011–1077] of the Song dynasty [960–1279], and I should pass the number on to you." So, I took the old man home and told my mother about this. Mother advised me to treat him well. She also said since this man was proficient in the principle of destiny, I should ask him to calculate the number for me to see if it would work. I subsequently tested Mr. Kong's calculations, although they were about small things, but all accurate and effective.

余遂启读书之念，谋之表兄沈称，言："郁海谷先生，在沈友夫家开馆，我送汝寄学甚便。"余遂礼郁为师。孔为余起数：县考童生，当十四名；府考七十一名，提学考第九名。明年赴考，三处名数皆合。

After hearing Mr. Kong's advice, I resumed the idea of scholarly study and discussed it with my cousin Shen Cheng, he said: "My good friend Mr. Yu Haigu opened a school at Shen Youfu's house. It is very convenient for me to send you there to stay and study." I thereafter greeted Mr. Yu Haigu as my teacher. Mr. Kong once calculated my destiny numbers: when I was still a pupil, I would be ranked 14th in the county exam, 71st in the prefectural exam, and 9th in the provincial exam. In the following year, my rankings in the three exams exactly matched what Mr. Kong had predicted.

复为卜终身休咎，言：某年考第几名，某年当补廪，某年当贡，贡后某年，当选四川一大尹，在任三年半，即宜告归。五十三岁八月十四日丑时，当终于正寝，惜无子。余备录而谨记之。

Mr. Kong also calculated the number of good and bad lucks in my life, he said: "In a certain year, you would be ranked a certain number in the Imperial Examination; in a certain year, you would be a stipend student; in a certain year, you would be an Imperial College student; and in a certain year after the Imperial College, you would be elected as the county magistrate of Sichuan province. After 3.5 years in the office, you would resign and return to your hometown. When you reach the age of 53 on the 14th lunar day of the 8th lunar month, you pass away. It was a pity that you did not have children." I carefully recorded these words and kept them in my mind.

自此以后，凡遇考校，其名数先后，皆不出孔公所悬定者。独算余食廪米九十一石五斗当出贡；及食米七十一石，屠宗师即批准补贡，余窃疑之。后果为署印杨公所驳，直至丁卯年（公元1567年），殷秋溟宗师见余场中备卷，叹曰："五策，即五篇奏议也，岂可使博洽淹贯之儒，老于窗下乎！"遂依县申文准贡，连前食米计之，实九十一石五斗也。余因此益信进退有命，迟速有时，澹然无求矣。

From then on, whenever there was an exam, my ranking would not be outside Mr. Kong's estimation, except that when I had eaten 91 *dan/shi* and 5 *dou* of rice, I would be out of the Imperial College. Who would know that when I had eaten 71 *dan* of rice, my application for a stipend was approved by Master Tu (Director of Education). I secretly suspected that Mr. Kong's calculation was somewhat inaccurate. Later, as expected, my grant application was rejected by another director, Master Yang, and I was not allowed to be a stipend student until the year of Dingmao (1567) when Master Yin Qiuming saw that I had failed the "Alternative test paper" in the exam room. He felt sorry for me and sighed: "The five strategies in this paper are like a memorial to the throne. How could such an erudite scholar be buried until old age?" Then he ordered the county magistrate to approve my grant application and compensated me as a stipend student. After all these twists and turns, I was supplied with more rice for an extended period. Counting the 71 *dan* that I had eaten before, the total was 91 *dan* and 5 *dou*. I therefore believed even more so that one's advance and retreat in fame and fortune were all predestined, and that there was a time when one could get lucky, so I took everything lightly and stopped pursuing it.

贡入燕都，留京一年，终日静坐，不阅文字。己巳（公元 1569 年）归，游南雍，未入监，先访云谷会禅师于栖霞山中，对坐一室，凡三昼夜不瞑目。

According to the regulations, after being selected as a stipend student, I had to study at the Imperial College in the capital city of Beijing for a year. Sitting quietly all day long, I was neither thinking nor talking, not even reviewing literature. In the year of Jisi (1569), I returned to Nanjing to study at the Imperial College there. Before entering the Imperial College, I went to Qixia Mountain to meet Chan/Zen Master Yungu (lit. "Cloud Valley"), who was an accomplished monk. I sat with him face to face in a Chan room for 3 days and 3 nights without closing my eyes.

云谷问曰："凡人所以不得作圣者，只为妄念相缠耳。汝坐三日，不见起一妄念，何也？"余曰："吾为孔先生算定，荣辱生死，皆有定数，即要妄想，亦无可妄想。"云谷笑曰："我待汝是豪杰，原来只是凡夫。"

Master Yungu inquired: "The reason that an ordinary person cannot become a sage is because their mind is constantly entangled with delusions. You have been sitting in meditation for 3 days, but I have not seen you having a delusion. Why?" I replied: "My destiny has been calculated by Mr. Kong about when I will receive honor or dishonor, and when I will die, it is all predetermined. Even if I think about benefit, it will be in vain; if I don't think about it, there will be no delusional thoughts in my mind." Master Yungu commented with a smile: "I thought you were an exceptional person, but you turn out to be just an ordinary person."

问其故？曰："人未能无心，终为阴阳所缚，安得无数？但惟凡人有数；极善之人，数固拘他不定；极恶之人，数亦拘他不定。汝二十年来，被他算定，不曾转动一毫，岂非是凡夫？"

I asked what he meant, Master Yungu replied: "An ordinary person cannot have an unconscious mind without delusional thoughts; so, they will be constantly restrained by the *yin yang* forces, how can they not have destiny numbers? Only ordinary people are bound by their destiny numbers. For those extremely kind people, destiny numbers will not hold them back. Even if very kind people are destined to suffer hardships, if they have done great good deeds, they can turn suffering into good fortune. For those extremely evil people, destiny numbers will also not work for them. Even if very evil people are destined to enjoy themselves, if they have done extremely evil deeds, they can turn blessing into misfortune. Your destiny number has been calculated by Mr. Kong for 20 years; the number has held you captive and you haven't changed the number even a little bit. Aren't you an ordinary person?"

余问曰："然则数可逃乎？"曰："命由我作，福自己求。诗书所称，的为明训。我教典中说：'求富贵得富贵，求男女得男女，求长寿得长寿。'夫妄语乃释迦大戒，诸佛菩萨，岂诳语欺人？"

I asked Master Yungu: "Then, can I escape my destiny number?" He replied: "I create my own destiny and seek my own blessings. Classic poetry books say so, and it is indeed wise admonition. Our Buddhist scriptures state: 'If one asks for wealth, they will gain wealth; if one asks for children, they will have children; and if one asks for longevity, they will increase longevity.' Since telling lies is a great precept of Buddhism, how could Buddha and Bodhisattva tell lies to deceive others?"

余进曰："孟子言：'求则得'，是求在我者也。道德仁义可以力求；功名富贵，如何求得？"云谷曰："孟子之言不错，汝自错解耳。汝不见六祖说：'一切福田，不离方寸；从心而觅，感无不通。' 求在我，不独得道德仁义，亦得功名富贵；内外双得，是求有益于得也。若不反躬内省，而徒向外驰求，则求之有道，而得之有命矣，内外双失，故无益。"

I inquired further: "Mengzi [Mencius, 372–289 BCE] said: 'Whatever you seek, you can get it.' It means that I can seek whatever in my heart: Virtue, benevolence, and righteousness are all in my heart that I can try my best to pursue. But fame, wealth, and honor are not in my heart that can only be obtained if others give them to me, how can I ask for these?" Master Yungu replied: "Mengzi's words are correct, but your explanation is wrong. Didn't you hear that the Sixth Patriarch Master Huineng [lit. "Capable of Wisdom"] said: 'All good fortunes are determined in one's heart. If you pray for blessings from your heart, there is nothing that you cannot induce to access.' If you seek them correctly in your heart, you can not only gain virtue, benevolence, and righteousness, but also fame, wealth, and honor, which are called internal and external gains. Your search will benefit from the gains. If you cannot examine and reflect on why you seek them, but only blindly pursue fame, wealth, and honor from the external environment, then there is a way to seek them, and there is a destiny to get them. If you seek fame, wealth, and honor that you are not destined to get, you will lose all the virtue, benevolence, and righteousness in your heart. Wouldn't that be a loss both internally and externally? Thus, there is no benefit in seeking them."

因问："孔公算汝终身若何？"余以实告。云谷曰："汝自揣应得科第否？应生子否？"余追省良久，曰："不应也。科第中人，类有福相，余福薄，又不能积功累行，以基厚福；兼不耐烦剧，不能容人；时或以才智盖人，直心直行，轻言妄谈。凡此皆薄福之相也，岂宜科第哉。

Master Yungu then asked me: "What destiny number did Mr. Kong calculate for you?" I told him truthfully. Master Yungu said: "Think about it for yourself, should you obtain honor in the Imperial Examination? Should you have children?" I reflected on it for a while and said: "I should not have these. Those people who have obtained honor in the Imperial Examinations have fortunate looks. My blessings are few, I cannot accumulate enough merits or good deeds to build a foundation for great blessings. And I am intolerant of others' shortcomings. Sometimes I am arrogant and put my talents and intelligence above those of others. I talk and behave too bluntly. All these characters are signs of fewer blessings. How can I obtain honor in the Imperial Examination?

地之秽者多生物，水之清者常无鱼；余好洁，宜无子者一；和气能育万物，余善怒，宜无子者二；爱为生生之本，忍为不育之根；余矜惜名节，常不能舍己救人，宜无子者三； 多言耗气，宜无子者四；喜饮铄精，宜无子者五； 好彻夜长坐，而不知葆元毓神，宜无子者六。其馀过恶尚多，不能悉数。"

Dirty soil can often grow more organisms, crystal clear water often cannot support fish; I love cleanliness too much, which is the first reason that I don't have children. Harmony can nurture all things; I get angry often, which is the second reason I don't have children. Love is the basis of life, cruelty is the root of infertility; I only cherish my own fame, but I am unwilling to sacrifice myself to rescue others, which is the third reason I don't have children. Overtalking can consume one's energy; I talk too much, which is the fourth reason I don't have children. Drinking alcohol can disperse one's spirit; I enjoy drinking too much, which is the fifth reason I don't have children. Sitting all nights cannot maintain one's vitality, which is the sixth reason I don't have children. I have made many other mistakes, too many to mention."

云谷曰:"岂惟科第哉。世间享千金之产者,定是千金人物;享百金之产者,定是百金人物;应饿死者,定是饿死人物;天不过因材而笃,几曾加纤毫意思。

Master Yungu said: "Not only are you undeserving of honor in the Imperial Examination; whether you are blessed or not is all determined by your own heart. In this world, those who enjoy the blessing of a thousand pieces of gold must be those who deserve a thousand pieces of gold; those who enjoy the blessing of a hundred pieces of gold must be those who deserve a hundred pieces of gold; and those who suffer the retribution of starvation must be those who deserve deadly starvation. Heaven only treats each person according to their own good or evil qualities and allows them to get the rewards they deserve. Heaven never adds the slightest thought of its own love or hate.

即如生子,有百世之德者,定有百世子孙保之;有十世之德者,定有十世子孙保之;有三世二世之德者,定有三世二世子孙保之;其斩焉无后者,德至薄也。

Like giving birth to a son, it all depends on the kind of seed you sow. If you sow plenty, you will reap plenty. If you sow thinly, you will reap thinly. If you have accumulated virtues for a hundred generations, you will have a hundred generations to protect your good fortune. If you have accumulated virtues for ten generations, you will have ten generations to protect your good fortune. If you have accumulated virtues for three or two generations, you will have three or two generations to protect your good fortune. Those who only enjoy one generation of good fortune are because their virtues are very small.

汝今既知非。将向来不发科第，及不生子之相，尽情改刷；务要积德，务要包荒，务要和爱，务要惜精神。从前种种，譬如昨日死；从后种种，譬如今日生；此义理再生之身。

Since you know your shortcomings, you should do your best to change the various disadvantages that have caused you to be unable to obtain honor or have children. You must accumulate virtues, you must be loving and compassionate toward others, you must embrace others, and you must cherish your own spirit. Everything in the past, like yesterday, has gone; everything from now on, like today, has just begun. Being able to do this means that you have been reborn as a benevolent and righteous person.

夫血肉之身，尚然有数；义理之身，岂不能格天。太甲曰：'天作孽，犹可违；自作孽，不可活。' 诗云：'永言配命，自求多福。' 孔先生算汝不登科第，不生子者，此天作之孽，犹可得而违；汝今扩充德性，力行善事，多积阴德，此自己所作之福也，安得而不受享乎？

Our bodies of flesh and blood certainly have destiny numbers; as for our benevolent spirits, can we not touch heaven? *The Book of Documents'* (*Shang Shu*) Taijia Chapter says that 'A natural disaster may be avoided; but if malevolent people do evil themselves, they will receive retribution and not be able to live happily in this world.' *The Classic of Poetry* also suggests that 'always align your behavior with the laws of nature when pursuing a happy life, it is up to you to decide whether you seek good or misfortune.' Mr. Kong calculated that you were destined to have no honor or children. But you can change these. If you improve your inherent virtues, do as many good deeds as possible, and secretly accumulate more hidden virtues, all of which will increase your blessings that others cannot take away, how can you not enjoy doing these?

易为君子谋，趋吉避凶；若言天命有常，吉何可趋，凶何可避？开章第一义，便说：'积善之家，必有馀庆。'汝信得及否？"

The Book of Changes (*Yi Jing*) also presents strategies for virtuous people to align their behaviors with the auspicious side and to avoid dangerous places and people. If one's destiny cannot be changed, how can good fortune be followed and misfortune be avoided? The first chapter in the *Book of Changes* says that 'a family that accumulates good deeds will have abundant celebrations.' Don't you believe this?"

余信其言，拜而受教。因将往日之罪，佛前尽情发露，为疏一通，先求登科；誓行善事三千条，以报天地祖宗之德。

I believed what Master Yungu said, thanked him, and accepted his advice. Thereafter, I revealed in front of Buddha all the mistakes, big and small, that I made in the past. I also wrote an article, first to pray for honor, and then to promise to do 3,000 good deeds to repay the great kindness of heaven, earth, and ancestors for giving birth to me.

云谷出功过格示余，令所行之事，逐日登记；善则记数，恶则退除，且教持准提咒，以期必验。

Master Yungu heard this, he showed me the merit and demerit grid book, and asked me to record my deeds every day, good and bad, according to the categorization method in the grid book. If I did bad deeds, depending on their severity, my recorded merits would be deducted. Master Yungu also taught me how to recite Cundi Mantra to enhance the power of Buddha to make my wishes come true.

语余曰:"符箓家有云:'不会书符,被鬼神笑。'此有秘传,只是不动念也。执笔书符,先把万缘放下,一尘不起。从此念头不动处,下一点,谓之混沌开基。由此而一笔挥成,更无思虑,此符便灵。凡祈天立命,都要从无思无虑处感格。

Master Yungu then said: "An expert who could draw talismans once declared: 'If you cannot draw a talisman, you will be ridiculed by demons.' There is a secret method of drawing talisman that has been passed down, which is a matter of not thinking about it. When holding the pen to draw the talisman, you should let go of even a trace of distracting thought, otherwise your mind will not be pure. When your thought is still, mark a point on the paper, call it creating a foundation from chaos, from which a complete talisman can be drawn without thinking, then this talisman will be very effective. When you pray to heaven to establish your destiny, you must work very hard to eliminate delusion to move heaven.

孟子论立命之学,而曰:'夭寿不贰。'夫夭寿,至贰者也。当其不动念时,孰为夭,孰为寿?细分之,丰歉不贰,然后可立贫富之命;穷通不贰,然后可立贵贱之命;夭寿不贰,然后可立生死之命。人生世间,惟死生为重,曰夭寿,则一切顺逆皆该之矣。

Mengzi discussed the principle of establishing destiny and said: 'There is no difference between a short life and a long life.' Does it sound strange at first? Because short life and long life are completely opposite. You should know that when you have no delusion, you are like a fetus in utero, how can you know the difference between short life and long life? If we scrutinize the two words "establishing destiny," the rich and the poor should be regarded as the same. Even if you are poor, you should still do good to transform your destiny. There is no difference between poverty and prosperity; those who are underdeveloped should still do good, eliminate evil, and sow seeds of blessing. There is no difference between a short life and a long life; do not do evil to ruin a life even if it is destined to be short. In this world, only life is the most important thing. Since short life and long life are the same, the good and the bad in everything should be embraced.

至修身以俟之，乃积德祈天之事。曰修，则身有过恶，皆当治而去之；曰俟，则一毫觊觎，一毫将迎，皆当斩绝之矣。到此地位，直造先天之境，即此便是实学。

Regarding cultivating your character to wait for something, it means that you should accumulate virtues and pray to heaven. Cultivation indicates that you have some faults that should be treated as a disease to be completely cut off. Regarding waiting for something, you should remove any trace of thought about welcoming something that does not belong to you. To be able to do this, you have reached the state of innate stillness of thought, which is real knowledge that can be used in the world.

汝未能无心，但能持准提咒，无记无数，不令间断，持得纯熟，于持中不持，于不持中持。到得念头不动，则灵验矣。"

You have not yet achieved the state of innate stillness of thought, but if you can recite the Cundi Mantra without memorizing it, counting it, or interrupting it, you will be very familiar with the mantra. You can recite it in your mouth without feeling it or recite it in your heart without realizing it. This is called holding on to the recitation without reciting it. If you can recite the mantra on this level, the self, the mantra, and the thought will become one, and no distracting thought will come to your mind, the mantra will then be very effective."

余初号学海，是日改号了凡；盖悟立命之说，而不欲落凡夫窠臼也。从此而后，终日兢兢，便觉与前不同。前日只是悠悠放任，到此自有战兢惕厉景象，在暗室屋漏中，常恐得罪天地鬼神；遇人憎我毁我，自能恬然容受。

My birth name was Xuehai (lit. "Sea of Learning"), but from that day onwards, I changed my name to Liaofan (lit. "Cease being Ordinary"), as I began to know the principle of destiny and did not want to be an ordinary person, so I swept away all the opinions of ordinary people. From then on, I had been very cautious all day long every day and had felt very different from my old self. Previously, I was carefree about everything; but then, I became naturally cautious and respectful of all things. Even in a darkroom with no one else around, I was often afraid of offending heaven, earth, or divine spirit. When I encountered those people who hated me or slandered me, I could accept it calmly without arguing with them.

到明年（公元1570年）礼部考科举，孔先生算该第三，忽考第一；其言不验，而秋闱中式矣。然行义未纯，检身多误；或见一善而行之不勇，或救人而心常自疑；或身勉为善，而口有过言；或醒时操持，而醉后放逸；以过折功，日常虚度。自己巳岁（公元1569年）发愿，直至己卯岁（公元1579年），历十馀年，而三千善行始完。

In the following year (1570), I went to take the Imperial Examination at the Ministry of Rites. Mr. Kong foretold that I should be ranked 3rd, but I was ranked 1st. His words began to be ineffective. When the provincial exam came in the fall, I passed it again. Although I had corrected many of my mistakes, after reflection, I still had many more mistakes to correct. For example, although I was willing to do good when seeing it, I was unable to forge ahead with all my courage and conviction. When it came to saving others, I often had doubts in my heart. When I reluctantly did good, I often said wrong things. When I was awake, I could control myself, but when I was drunk, I acted recklessly. My accumulated merits might not be enough to make up for my mistakes, and my time was often wasted. For over a decade, from the year of Jisi (1569) to the year of Jimao (1579), I completed 3,000 good deeds.

时方从李渐庵入关，未及回向。庚辰（公元 1580 年）南还。始请性空，慧空诸上人，就东塔禅堂回向。遂起求子愿，亦许行三千善事。辛巳（公元 1581 年），生男天启。

Then, I followed Mr. Li Jian'an to return from the border, but I did not have time to transfer my merit. In the year of Gengchen (1580), I returned to the south from Beijing, and invited two accomplished Buddhist monks, Xingkong (lit. "Empty Heart") and Huikong (lit. "Empty Mind"), to fulfill my wish of merit transfer in the Chan Hall of East Pagoda. Then, I had another wish to have a child and made a big promise to do another 3,000 good deeds. In the year of Xinsi (1581), my son was born, named Tianqi (lit. "Heavenly Revelation").

余行一事，随以笔记；汝母不能书，每行一事，辄用鹅毛管，印一朱圈于历日之上。或施食贫人，或买放生命，一日有多至十馀者。至癸未（公元 1583 年）八月，三千之数已满。复请性空辈，就家庭回向。九月十三日，复起求中进士愿，许行善事一万条，丙戌（公元 1586 年）登第，授宝坻知县。

Every time I did a good deed, I would write it down in a notebook. My wife (Your mother, referring to his son) could not write, so every time I did a good deed, she would use a goose quill pen to mark a red circle on the calendar, or send food to the poor, or buy living things to release them. Sometimes there were more than a dozen red circles a day to indicate that I had done over a dozen good deeds in one day. In the 8th lunar month of the Guiwei year

(1583), I fulfilled my wish of completing another 3,000 good deeds. Then I reinvited the accomplished Buddhist monk Xingkong and others to my home to transfer my merit. On the 13th lunar day of the 9th lunar month of that year, I made another wish to become a Jinshi [highest and final degree in the Imperial Examination, equivalent to today's Doctorate], and to do another 10,000 good deeds. In the Bingxu year (1586), I attained the Jinshi degree, so the Ministry of Personnel filled my vacated position of magistrate at Baodi county.

余置空格一册，名曰治心篇。晨起坐堂，家人携付门役，置案上，所行善恶，纤悉必记。夜则设桌于庭，效赵阅道焚香告帝。

When I was the county magistrate, I prepared a blank notebook, "Curing the Heart." Every morning when I got up and sat in court to hear the cases, I would ask a family member to bring the notebook and pass it on to the gatekeeper to place it on my desk. My good and bad deeds, even if very small, must be recorded in the notebook every day. Every evening, we would set up a table in the courtyard, imitating Zhao Yuedao (1008–1084) to burn incense and pray to gods.

汝母见所行不多，辄颦蹙曰："我前在家，相助为善，故三千之数得完；今许一万，衙中无事可行，何时得圆满乎？"

When my wife [your mother, talking to his son] saw that I did not do a lot of good deeds, she often frowned and said: "I used to help you do good deeds at home, so you could fulfill your wish of completing 3,000. Now you have made a promise to do another 10,000 good deeds, but there is nothing to do in the office, how long will it take before you can finish them all?"

夜间偶梦见一神人，余言善事难完之故。神曰："只减粮一节，万行俱完矣。" 盖宝坻之田，每亩二分三厘七毫。余为区处，减至一分四厘六毫，委有此事，心颇惊疑。适幻余禅师自五台来，余以梦告之，且问此事宜信否？

That night, I accidentally dreamed of seeing a deity, and explained to him why it was difficult to complete the 10,000 good deeds. The deity said: "Just because you reduced the payable amount of grain for the commoners when you were the county magistrate, you have already done the 10,000 good deeds." It turned out that the land in Baodi county was charged 2 *fen* 3 *li* and 7 *hao* per *mu*. I felt the people paid too much tax, so I measured up all the land in the county and reduced the payable amount of grain to 1 *fen* 4 *li* and 6 *hao* per *mu*. This incident indeed occurred, but I wondered how the deity knew about this. Coincidentally, Chan Master Huanyu (lit. "Illusion Lingering") came from Mount Wutai (lit. "Five Terraces"), I told him about the dream and asked him, "Should I believe this?"

师曰："善心真切，即一行可当万善，况合县减粮，万民受福乎？" 吾即捐俸银，请其就五台山斋僧一万而回向之。

Master Huanyu said: "When doing good deeds, you must be sincere and not to be double-faced. Then even one good deed is worth 10,000 good deeds. Moreover, when you reduced the payable amount of grain for the entire county people, all the farmers have benefited from your tax reduction and relieved from the pain of heavy taxes, the people have thus received many blessings!" After hearing the Master's words, I immediately donated my salary and asked him to transfer it to 10,000 monks in Mount Wutai, and I would also transfer the merits of the monks' lives.

孔公算予五十三岁有厄，余未尝祈寿，是岁竟无恙，今六十九矣。书曰："天难谌，命靡常。"又云："惟命不于常"，皆非诳语。吾于是而知，凡称祸福自己求之者，乃圣贤之言。若谓祸福惟天所命，则世俗之论矣。

Mr. Kong predicted that there would be a disaster when I turned 53 years old. Although I did not pray for longevity, I did not have any problem when I was 53. And now, I am 69. *The Book of Documents* says: "Do not easily believe in heaven, as one's destiny is often uncertain." It also says: "People's lives are inconstant," which are not at all false statements. From this I know that the maxims about misfortunes and good fortunes all sought by the people themselves are the words of sages. If some say that misfortunes and good fortunes are all predestined, these are the words of common folks.

汝之命，未知若何？即命当荣显，常作落寞想；即时当顺利，常作拂逆想；即眼前足食，常作贫窭想；即人相爱敬，常作恐惧想；即家世望重，常作卑下想；即学问颇优，常作浅陋想。

How is your destiny? Even if you are destined to be glorious and dignified, you often think that you are lonely and living in poverty. Even if things go smoothly, you often think that you are facing adversity. Even if you have plenty of food, you often think that you are poor. Even if others like you and respect you, you are often cautious and fearful. Even if your family has been famous for generations, you are often humble. Even if you have profound knowledge, you often think you are superficial.

远思扬祖宗之德，近思盖父母之愆；上思报国之恩，下思造家之福；外思济人之急，内思闲己之邪。

When talking about the distant past, you should think about promoting the virtues of your ancestors. When talking about immediate matters, you should think about avoiding your parents' mistakes. When talking about advancement, you should think about serving the country. When talking about retreat, you should think about making your family happy. When talking about external affairs, you should think about relieving the emergencies of others. When talking about internal matters, you should think about preventing evil thought.

务要日日知非，日日改过；一日不知非，即一日安于自是；一日无过可改，即一日无步可进；天下聪明俊秀不少，所以德不加修，业不加广者，只为因循二字，耽阁一生。

People should know that they make mistakes every day and they must correct them every day. If they do not know their mistakes every day, they may be content with themselves every day. If there is nothing to correct every day, there is no progress every day. There are many clever and good-looking people in the world, but they are unwilling to cultivate their virtues, and they do not advance their careers, just because they follow conformity and waste their lives.

云谷禅师所授立命之说，乃至精至邃，至真至正之理，其熟玩而勉行之，毋自旷也。

Chan Master Yungu's teaching about establishing destiny is precise, profound, true, and correct. I hope you [his son] study it carefully, do your best to adhere to it, and do not waste your precious time.

了凡四训·第二章·改过之法

Liaofan's Four Lessons
Lesson 2: Ways to Correct Oneself

春秋诸大夫，见人言动，亿而谈其祸福，靡不验者，左国诸记可观也。大都吉凶之兆，萌乎心而动乎四体，其过于厚者常获福，过于薄者常近祸，俗眼多翳，谓有未定而不可测者。至诚合天，福之将至，观其善而必先知之矣。祸之将至，观其不善而必先知之矣。今欲获福而远祸，未论行善，先须改过。

In the Spring and Autumn period (770–476 BCE), senior officials often predicted one's good or misfortune by observing their words and deeds, and it was often accurate. These records can be found in books such as Zuozhuan (*The Tradition of Zuo*) and Guoyu (*Discourses of the States*). All auspicious and inauspicious omens come from the heart and are reflected in the body and limbs. An extremely kind person with a stable body and limbs is always blessed. An extremely mean person with a frivolous body and limbs is often in trouble. Ordinary people mostly have blocked visions, and they say that good and bad fortunes are uncertain and unpredictable. Those who are extremely sincere, their hearts are in harmony with heaven. When you observe a person and see their good deeds, you can predict that their good fortune will naturally arrive. When you observe a person and see their bad deeds, you can predict that their misfortune will eventually come. If people want to be blessed and stay away from disasters, they must first correct their mistakes before talking about doing good deeds.

但改过者，第一，要发耻心。思古之圣贤，与我同为丈夫，彼何以百世可师？我何以一身瓦裂？耽染尘情，私行不义，谓人不知，傲然无愧，将日沦于禽兽而不自知矣；世之可羞可耻者，莫大乎此。孟子曰：耻之于人大矣。以其得之则圣贤，失之则禽兽耳。此改过之要机也。

The first way to correct oneself is to have a sense of shame. Think about ancient sages who were all men like me. Why can they be celebrated as role models for centuries? Why am I broken in this life? It is because I am polluted by the environment, secretly seeking indulgence in sensual enjoyment and desire satisfaction, doing all sorts of things I shouldn't do, and thinking that others don't know. I have no regard for the rules or sense of shame. I just keep sinking like an animal without knowing it myself. There is no greater shame than this in the world. Mengzi said: "The most important thing for a person to learn is shame." If one knows shame, they will correct their mistakes and may become a sage; otherwise, they may act recklessly like an animal. This is the crucial secret to self-correction.

第二，要发畏心。天地在上，鬼神难欺，吾虽过在隐微，而天地鬼神，实鉴临之，重则降之百殃，轻则损其现福，吾何可以不惧？不惟此也。闲居之地，指视昭然；吾虽掩之甚密，文之甚巧，而肺肝早露，终难自欺；被人觑破，不值一文矣，乌得不懔懔？不惟是也。一息尚存，弥天之恶，犹可悔改；古人有一生作恶，临死悔悟，发一善念，遂得善终者。谓一念猛厉，足以涤百年之恶也。譬如千年幽谷，一灯才照，则千年之暗俱除；故过不论久近，惟以改为贵。但尘世无常，肉身易殒，一息不属，欲改无由矣。明则千百年担负恶名，虽孝子慈孙，不能洗涤；幽则千百劫沉沦狱报，虽圣贤佛菩萨，不能援引。乌得不畏？

The second way to correct oneself is to be cautious and fearful. Heaven and earth are above us, and the divine spirit is not easily deceived. Although I made the mistakes in secluded places, heaven, earth, and divine spirit are observing me and reflecting my mistakes like a mirror. If I made a big mistake, all sorts of disasters would befall me. If I made a small mistake, it would reduce my blessings. How can I not be fearful? It is not only this. Even in a secluded space at home, the divine spirit's observation is still very discerning. Although I have hidden my mistakes very carefully and covered them up skillfully, in the eyes of the divine, my lungs and liver have been seen through, and my faults are all exposed; there is no way to deceive myself. If others can see through me, I will be worthless. How can I not be cautious and fearful? It is not only that. If a person is alive, even if having committed to heinous evil, they can still repent and change. There was an ancient man who had done evil all his life, when he was dying, he suddenly repented and had a great kind thought and immediately had a good death. This means that if a person can come up with a very kind and courageous idea at a critical moment, they can cleanse their accumulated past mistakes. Just like a lamp lighting up a very dark valley, wherever the light reaches, it can completely remove the darkness of over 1,000 years. So, whether the mistake is old or new, if it is corrected, that is great. This impure world is disillusioned and impermanent. Our bodies of flesh and blood are easy to perish. If I cannot breathe for a moment, my body will no longer be mine, and there will be no way to correct anything even if I want to. The overt retribution will bring a person hundreds of years of bad reputation in the world, even if they have filial sons and loving grandsons who cannot cleanse their blemishes. The covert retribution will sink a person hundreds of years of suffering to the underworld, even if they meet sages, Buddhas, or Bodhisattvas who cannot save or guide them. How can we not be afraid?

第三，须发勇心。人不改过，多是因循退缩；吾须奋然振作，不用迟疑，不烦等待。小者如芒刺在肉，速与抉剔；大者如毒蛇啮指，速与斩除，无丝毫凝滞，此风雷之所以为益也。

The third way to correct oneself is to have the courage to move forward. A person refusing to correct their mistakes is mostly because they muddle along and fall backward. I must work hard without hesitation or delay and not wait for tomorrow. A small mistake is like a sharp thorn poking into the flesh that needs to be pulled out quickly. A big mistake is like a poisonous snake biting the finger that must be cut off immediately. These remediable actions are like when the wind blows and the thunder stirs, all things grow, and the benefits are great.

具是三心，则有过斯改，如春冰遇日，何患不消乎？然人之过，有从事上改者，有从理上改者，有从心上改者；工夫不同，效验亦异。

If one has the above-mentioned three types of mindsets: shame, fear, and courage, they will be able to correct their mistakes immediately, just like thin ice exposed to the sun in spring, who is worried about it not melting? Nevertheless, there are different ways to correct a mistake: correcting it from the matter of fact, correcting it from the principle, and correcting it from the mindset. Using different techniques, the effects will also be different.

如前日杀生，今戒不杀；前日怒詈，今戒不怒；此就其事而改之者也。强制于外，其难百倍，且病根终在，东灭西生，非究竟廓然之道也。

For example, the day before yesterday one killed a living thing, today they are prohibited from killing. The day before yesterday one was very angry and cursed someone, today they are forbidden to get angry. This is a method of correcting a mistake in the matter and they are prevented from repeating it. But it is a hundred times more difficult to stop doing it than to change it naturally. Moreover, the root cause of the mistake has not been removed and is still in the heart. Although it is suppressed for a while, it will be eventually exposed, just like a fire is extinguished in the east, it will reemerge in the west. After all, this is not a method of reform that will completely remove it.

善改过者，未禁其事，先明其理；如过在杀生，即思曰：上帝好生，物皆恋命，杀彼养己，岂能自安？且彼之杀也，既受屠割，复入鼎镬，种种痛苦，彻入骨髓；己之养也，珍膏罗列，食过即空，疏食菜羹，尽可充腹，何必戕彼之生，损己之福哉？又思血气之属，皆含灵知，既有灵知，皆我一体；纵不能躬修至德，使之尊我亲我，岂可日戕物命，使之仇我憾我于无穷也？一思及此，将有对食痛心，不能下咽者矣。

Those who are willing to correct their mistakes must first understand the reason why something cannot be done before they are prohibited from doing it. For example, if one's fault is killing a living thing, they must first think: "Heaven has the power of generating life, and every living organism cherishes its own life and is afraid of death. If I kill its life to nourish my body, how can I find inner peace?" And some organisms, although they have been killed, but are not completely dead, such as fish or crabs. Putting it into a frying pan and burning it when it is half alive, this kind of pain will penetrate to its marrow. To nourish people themselves, they fill their dining table with all kinds of precious and delicious food. Once eaten, the food becomes residue. One must know that people can still be full even if they eat vegetables and soups. Why do they have to kill the lives of others, and reduce their own blessings? Think again: "Everything with flesh and blood has sensitive spirit. Since they all have sensitive spirits, they are the same as me. Even if I cannot cultivate myself to a very high level of virtue to make them respect me or keep them close to me, how can I kill them every day to become their enemy and make them hate me endlessly?" If one can think of this, they will feel sorrowful and unable to swallow the meat and living things on their dining table.

如前日好怒，必思曰：人有不及，情所宜矜；悖理相干，于我何与？本无可怒者。又思天下无自是之豪杰，亦无尤人之学问；有不得，皆己之德未修，感未至也。吾悉以自反，则谤毁之来，皆磨炼玉成之地；我将欢然受赐，何怒之有？

For example, if one could not control their anger before, they should think: "Everyone has their strengths and weaknesses. When I encounter someone's shortcomings, I should empathize with them and forgive their mistakes. If someone offends me, it is their fault. What does it have to do with me? There is nothing to be angry about. Think again that there is no outstanding person in the world who praises themself, and there is no knowledge that specializes in criticizing others without knowing much about them. If one is dissatisfied with anything they do, it is because their virtues are not completely cultivated, their merits are not extensively accumulated, and their ability to move people's hearts is not enough. Everyone should reflect on themselves, then others' slander will become a venue for cultivation to temper them and improve their positive qualities. I shall happily learn the lessons that others teach me, or receive criticisms from others, so that I will have the chance to achieve greatness. Why should I get angry?"

又闻而不怒，虽谗焰薰天，如举火焚空，终将自息；闻谤而怒，虽巧心力辩，如春蚕作茧，自取缠绵；怒不惟无益，且有害也。其馀种种过恶，皆当据理思之。此理既明，过将自止。

One should be able to control their anger when hearing others saying bad things about them, although the wicked words can be as bad as using a torch to burn the sky, since there is nothing to burn in the void, the flame will eventually extinguish. If they get angry when hearing someone saying bad things about them, and they try their best to argue, the result is like making silk threads from silkworm cocoons that they may bind themself in the process. So, anger is not only useless, but also harmful. As for making other mistakes, one should think about all things carefully according to the principles. If they can understand the various principles, they will naturally stop making mistakes.

何谓从心而改？过有千端，惟心所造；吾心不动，过安从生？学者于好色，好名，好货，好怒，种种诸过，不必逐类寻求；但当一心为善，正念现前，邪念自然污染不上。如太阳当空，魍魉潜消，此精一之真传也。过由心造，亦由心改，如斩毒树，直断其根，奚必枝枝而伐，叶叶而摘哉？

What does it mean to correct mistakes from the heart? There are thousands upon thousands of faults, all generated from the heart. If my heart is unmoved, where can faults come from? Some scholars favor lust, fame, property, and can lose temper easily. For all these sorts of mistakes, there is no need to seek ways to eliminate them successively. If one does good deeds sincerely, righteous thoughts will appear, and evil thoughts will naturally not pollute them. It is like when the bright sun shines in the sky, all monsters will gradually disappear, this is the purest and only true secret of cultivating the heart and correcting mistakes. All mistakes are generated from the heart, and they should be corrected from the heart. Just like removing a poisonous tree completely, one must eradicate it by the roots. Why cut the branches off one by one, and pull the leaves off one by one?

大抵最上治心，当下清净；才动即觉，觉之即无；苟未能然，须明理以遣之；又未能然，须随事以禁之；以上事而兼行下功，未为失策。执下而昧上，则拙矣。

The best way to correct mistakes is to cure the heart, then one will immediately make their mind pure. They notice it whenever their bad thought arises, then they stop it immediately. If this is impossible, they must understand the principles and discard the thought of making such a mistake. If this is impossible, they must forcefully suppress it when making such a mistake. If they use high-level skills of curing the heart, and low-level skills of forcefully suppressing it when they are about to make such a mistake, this is not necessarily unwise. To insist on using only low-level skills but ignoring high-level skills, this is foolishness.

顾发愿改过，明须良朋提醒，幽须鬼神证明；一心忏悔，昼夜不懈，经一七，二七，以至一月，二月，三月，必有效验。

When they make a wish to correct their mistakes, they need a good friend to remind them when they are confused; covertly they need a divine spirit to prove it for them. They also need to repent wholeheartedly, day and night, never stop. After 7 days, 14 days, 1 month, 2 months, or 3 months of repentance like this, it will be effective.

或觉心神恬旷；或觉智慧顿开；或处冗沓而触念皆通；或遇怨仇而回嗔作喜；或梦吐黑物；或梦往圣先贤，提携接引；或梦飞步太虚；或梦幢幡宝盖，种种胜事，皆过消罪灭之象也。然不得执此自高，画而不进。

They may feel tranquil, deepened, and suddenly enlightened, or their mind is still clear and knowledgeable even if in trouble, or they can entirely control anger and feel happy even if encountering a rival, or they may dream of spitting out dirty things with foul smell, or dream of an ancient sage coming to lift them up and guide them through, or dream of flying into the vast sky, or dream of colorful flags and umbrellas decorated with rare treasures. All these good omens suggest that their mistakes are eliminated. But they should not be arrogant or block their path of making further progress just because they have encountered these good signs.

昔蘧伯玉当二十岁时，已觉前日之非而尽改之矣。至二十一岁，乃知前之所改，未尽也；及二十二岁，回视二十一岁，犹在梦中，岁复一岁，递递改之，行年五十，而犹知四十九年之非，古人改过之学如此。

In the Spring and Autumn period (770–476 BCE), there was a wise minister of Wei State, named Qu Boyu, who was already awaken to his past mistakes and tried to correct them at the age of 20. When he was 21, he felt his past mistakes were not completely corrected. When he was 22, he looked back to the past 21 years and felt it was like he was in a dream. Year after year, he gradually corrected all his past mistakes until he turned 50. Nevertheless, he still felt he made mistakes in the past 49 years. The ancients paid so much attention to the knowledge of correction.

吾辈身为凡流，过恶猬集，而回思往事，常若不见其有过者，心粗而眼翳也。然人之过恶深重者，亦有效验：或心神昏塞，转头即忘；或无事而常烦恼；或见君子而赧然相沮；或闻正论而不乐；或施惠而人反怨；或夜梦颠倒，甚则妄言失志；皆作孽之相也，苟一类此，即须奋发，舍旧图新，幸勿自误。

We are all ordinary people, and our mistakes are like hedgehog quills. Due to our ignorance, it often seems that we have not made mistakes when recalling back. But if one's mistakes are serious, there is evidence to show them. For example, their mind is confused or blocked, and they turn around and easily forget things; or they often worry about worthless things; or they feel embarrassed when seeing virtuous people; or they feel unhappy when hearing upright principles; or they give favor to others but receive resentment in return; or they have opposite dreams at night, even give incoherent speech and lose their normal appearance. All these abnormal phenomena are manifestations of their past mistakes. If one has any of the above conditions, immediately work hard to correct their past mistakes, open a new path in life, and do not delay themself.

了凡四训·第三章·积善之方
Liaofan's Four Lessons
Lesson 3: Ways to Accumulate Kindness

易曰:"积善之家,必有馀庆。"昔颜氏将以女妻叔梁纥,而历叙其祖宗积德之长,逆知其子孙必有兴者。孔子称舜之大孝,曰:"宗庙飨之,子孙保之,"皆至论也。试以往事徵之。

Yi Jing (*Book of Changes*) says: "A family that accumulates good deeds will have abundant celebrations." Formerly, the Yan Family wanted to betroth their daughter to Confucius' father. They mentioned everything that the Kong Family had done and predicted that the Kong Family's accumulated virtues would be long-lasting, and that the Kong Family's descendants would become prosperous. Later, Confucius was born. Confucius once praised Shun's extraordinary filial piety, and said: "With such great filial piety, not only the Shun Family's ancestors would enjoy his sacrifices, but also his descendants could protect his virtues." The Chen State of the Spring and Autumn period (770–476 BCE) was passed down from Shun's descendants, which was enough to prove that the Shun Family had prospered for a long time. These are true stories.

杨少师荣,建宁人。世以济渡为生,久雨溪涨,横流冲毁民居,溺死者顺流而下,他舟皆捞取货物,独少师曾祖及祖,惟救人,而货物一无所取,乡人嗤其愚。逮少师父生,家渐裕,有神人化为道者,语之曰:"汝祖父有阴功,子孙当贵显,宜葬某地。"遂依其所指而窆之,即今白兔坟也。后生少师,弱冠登第,位至三公,加曾祖,祖,父,如其官。子孙贵盛,至今尚多贤者。

Yang Rong, who served as an imperial assistant officer, was from Jianning, Fujian province. His family had made a living by ferrying across the river for generations. One day, it rained for so long that it made the streams swollen, the river surged, and the houses swept away. The drowned people continued to flow down the river, all the other boats went to retrieve goods floating in the river, only Yang's great-grandfather and grandfather went to rescue the victims without retrieving any goods. The villagers snickered at them for being fools. After the imperial assistant officer's father was born, the family gradually became affluent. There was an immortal who transformed into a Daoist sage, said to his father: "Your grandfather and father have accumulated many hidden merits, their descendants will surely be prosperous and in high official posts. You should bury them somewhere." After hearing this, his father buried his great-grandfather and grandfather at the place designated by the Daoist sage, now known as the White Rabbit Tomb. Later, the imperial assistant officer was born, attained Jinshi [equivalent to today's Doctorate] at the age of 20, and became one of the three imperial assistant officers. The emperor also posthumously awarded his great-grandfather, grandfather, and father the same official position as his. Their descendants were also successful; many are still very capable and virtuous to this day.

鄞人杨自惩，初为县吏，存心仁厚，守法公平。时县宰严肃，偶挞一囚，血流满前，而怒犹未息，杨跪而宽解之。宰曰："怎奈此人越法悖理，不由人不怒。"

Yang Zicheng, a native of Ningbo, Zhejiang province, once worked as an official in the county government. He was very kind-hearted, abided by the law and acted impartially. The county magistrate at the time was a severe and harsh man who once beat a prisoner until blood flowed to the floor, but the magistrate still could not calm down. Yang knelt to beg the magistrate to have mercy on the prisoner. The county magistrate said: "This prisoner does not abide by the law and violates the rules. How can he stop me from being angry?!"

自惩叩首曰："上失其道，民散久矣，如得其情，哀矜勿喜；喜且不可，而况怒乎？"宰为之霁颜。

Yang Zicheng kowtowed and said: "The rules are lost in the court, and the people's hearts have been misled for a long time. If this prisoner was found guilty, I would feel sorry for him, but I would not be happy just because the case had been completed and closed. Since it is immoral to feel happy, how can you get angry?" The county magistrate was moved by Yang Zicheng's words, his face immediately softened and ceased from anger.

家甚贫，馈遗一无所取，遇囚人乏粮，常多方以济之。一日，有新囚数人待哺，家又缺米；给囚则家人无食；自顾则囚人堪悯；与其妇商之。妇曰："囚从何来？"曰："自杭而来。沿路忍饥，菜色可掬。"因撤己之米，煮粥以食囚。

Although Yang Zicheng's family was very poor, he refused to accept anything others gave to him. When he met the prisoners who were short of food, he often obtained rice in many ways to help them. One day, several new prisoners came without eating anything, but his family was also lacking in rice. If he gave their insufficient rice to the prisoners, his family would not have much to eat. If he cared only about his own family, the prisoners would be very hungry. He discussed it with his wife, she asked him: "Where did the prisoners come from?" He said: "They came from Hangzhou and suffered from hunger along the way; their faces look as green as vegetables." Thus, the couple used some of their saved rice to make porridge for the prisoners to eat.

后生二子，长曰守陈，次曰守址，为南北吏部侍郎；长孙为刑部侍郎；次孙为四川廉宪，又俱为名臣；今楚亭，德政，亦其裔也。

Later, Yang Zicheng and his wife gave birth to two sons, the elder one was named Shouchen (lit. "Preserving the Old"), and the younger one was called Shouzhi (lit. "Preserving the Site"), who served as ministers of the Northern and Southern Ministry of Personnel. Their eldest grandson became a minister in the Ministry of Justice, and their youngest grandson served as a government inspector in Sichuan province. Their two sons and two grandsons were all well-known officials. Today, the two famous people, Chuting (lit. "Chu State Pavilion") and Dezheng (lit. "Virtuous Politics"), are both descendants of Yang Zicheng.

昔正统间，邓茂七倡乱于福建，士民从贼者甚众；朝廷起鄞县张都宪楷南征，以计擒贼，后委布政司谢都事，搜杀东路贼党；谢求贼中党附册籍，凡不附贼者，密授以白布小旗，约兵至日，插旗门首，戒军兵无妄杀，全活万人；后谢之子迁，中状元，为宰辅；孙丕，复中探花。

In the Zhengtong era (1436–1449) of the Ming dynasty, a bandit Deng Maoqi (?–1449) rebelled in Fujian province and gained many followers. Subsequently, the emperor appointed Zhang Duxian (Zhang Kai, 1399–1460), a native of the Yin county who had served as an imperial envoy, to march southward to catch them. Zhang used a strategy to capture Deng. Later, Zhang sent Xie, the Chief Secretary of Fujian, to search and capture the remaining bandits along the east route. But Xie refused to kill indiscriminately and looked for the list of people who were unaffiliated with the rebels, he secretly gave them a small white-cotton flag that they could place at their doors when the soldiers arrive, so that the soldiers would not kill them randomly. About 10,000 lives were saved in this way.

Later, Xie's son, Xie Qian (1449–1531), attained Zhuangyuan [the highest score on the highest level of the Imperial Examination] and became Grand Chancellor. His grandson, Xie Pi (1482–1556), was also ranked 3rd in the Imperial Exam.

莆田林氏，先世有老母好善，常作粉团施人，求取即与之，无倦色；一仙化为道人，每旦索食六七团。母日日与之，终三年如一日，乃知其诚也。因谓之曰："吾食汝三年粉团，何以报汝？府后有一地，葬之，子孙官爵，有一升麻子之数。"

An elderly mother in the Lin family of Putian county, Fujian province, liked to do good deeds. She often gave rice balls to the poor, and whoever asked for it, she would give them immediately without showing any sign of tiredness. There was an immortal who transformed into a Daoist sage, and who asked her for six or seven rice balls every morning. The old lady gave him the rice balls every day for 3 years continuously. The immortal then knew her sincerity. He said to her: "I have eaten your rice balls for 3 years; how can I repay you? There is a piece of land behind your house, if you will be buried on this site after your passing, your descendants will have as many official titles as one liter of linseeds."

其子依所点葬之，初世即有九人登第，累代簪缨甚盛，福建有无林不开榜之谣。

After the old lady died, her sons buried her on the site designated by the Daoist sage. There were nine lineal descendants in the first generation of the Lin family who had passed the Imperial Examination. From generation to generation, many of the Lin family descendants became high-ranking officials. Thus, there was a popular saying in Fujian province that, "If there wasn't any Lin family member taking the Imperial Exam, the results would not be announced." It means that many people from the Lin family clan had taken the Imperial

Exam, and when the results were released, there were always people with the last name Lin on the list. It also indicates that many of the Lin family descendants had achieved their career success.

冯琢庵太史之父，为邑庠生。隆冬早起赴学，路遇一人，倒卧雪中，扪之，半僵矣。遂解己绵裘衣之，且扶归救苏。梦神告之曰："汝救人一命，出至诚心，吾遣韩琦为汝子。"及生琢庵，遂名琦。

When the father of the court historian Feng Zhuo'an was a scholar in the county school, on a very cold winter morning on his way to school, he saw a man lying in the snow. He touched him with his hands and found him almost freezing to death. The father immediately took off his own leather robe, put it on the dying man, brought him home, and saved his life. Later in a dream, a deity told the father: "You saved someone's life out of a sincere heart, I will send Han Qi [1008–1075, a Song-dynasty Grand Chancellor who was virtuous and versatile in both civil and military affairs] to be reincarnated as your son." Then Zhuo'an was born, named Feng Qi (1558–1603).

台州应[大猷]尚书，壮年习业于山中。夜鬼啸集，往往惊人，公不惧也；一夕闻鬼云："某妇以夫久客不归，翁姑逼其嫁人。明夜当缢死于此，吾得代矣。"

Minister Ying Dayou (1487–1581) in Taizhou, Zhejiang province studied in the mountains in his prime. At night, ghosts often gathered to make noises to scare people. Only Ying was not afraid of the noises. One evening, Ying heard a ghost saying: "There was a woman whose husband was away on a trip and had not returned for a long time. Her parents-in-law assumed that their son might be dead and forced her to remarry, but she refused. Tomorrow night, she will hang herself here, and I must find a substitute."

公潜卖田，得银四两。即伪作其夫之书，寄银还家；其父母见书，以手迹不类，疑之。既而曰："书可假，银不可假，想儿无恙。"妇遂不嫁。其子后归，夫妇相保如初。

Ying Dayou was moved by the woman's integrity and secretly sold his paddy field for four taels of silver. He immediately wrote a letter to the woman, pretending to be her husband, and sent her the money. After reading the letter, her parents-in-law suspected that the letter was fake because the handwriting did not look like their son's. But then they said: "The letter can be fake, but the money cannot be counterfeit, our son must be safe to send the money back." Afterwards, the parents-in-law no longer forced her to remarry. Later, when their son came back, the couple reunited and lived a happy life as newlyweds.

公又闻鬼语曰："我当得代，奈此秀才坏吾事。"旁一鬼曰："尔何不祸之？"曰："上帝以此人心好，命作阴德尚书矣，吾何得而祸之？"

On the following night, Ying Dayou heard again the ghost saying: "I could have found a substitute, but how could I know that this scholar would ruin my business?!" Another ghost beside said: "Why don't you kill him?" The first ghost said: "Heaven sent him to be the minister of hidden virtues because of his good heart; how can I kill him?"

应公因此益自努励，善日加修，德日加厚；遇岁饥，辄捐谷以赈之；遇亲戚有急，辄委曲维持；遇有横逆，辄反躬自责，怡然顺受；子孙登科第者，今累累也。

Thereafter, Ying Dayou worked even harder. He did good deeds every day and increased his virtues every day. When he encountered the year of famine, he donated grain to help others. When his relatives were in urgent need of something, he would try his best to help them. When he met unreasonable people, he would always reflect on and blame himself for the mistakes and calmly accept the facts. Ying's virtues had passed down to his descendants; today many of them have gained fame and official positions.

常熟徐凤竹栻，其父素富，偶遇年荒，先捐租以为同邑之倡，又分谷以赈贫乏，夜闻鬼唱于门曰："千不诳，万不诳；徐家秀才，做到了举人郎。"相续而呼，连夜不断。是岁，凤竹果举于乡，其父因而益积德，孳孳不怠，修桥修路，斋僧接众，凡有利益，无不尽心。后又闻鬼唱于门曰："千不诳，万不诳；徐家举人，直做到都堂。"凤竹官终两浙巡抚。

During the Ming dynasty (1368–1644), there was a gentleman named Xu Fengzhu in Changshu county, Jiangsu province. Fengzhu was his given name, he styled himself as "Shi." His father was very rich. When there was a year of famine, he would first donate all the rents he had collected from the land tenants, setting a good example for all the landowners in the county, then he would distribute his grain to help the poor. One night, he heard a group of ghosts singing at his gate: "Never lie even once, never lie even once, the scholar of the Xu family is about to succeed in the Imperial Exam." The ghosts kept singing, all night long. That year, Xu Fengzhu indeed passed the provincial examination. His father thus worked even more tirelessly to do good deeds and accumulate virtues. He built bridges, paved roads, and gave food to monks, if it was beneficial to the public, he would do it with all his heart. Later, he heard again the group of ghosts singing at his gate: "Never lie even once, never lie even once, the Juren [rank achieved by those who passed the provincial exam] of the Xu family will become an official in the capital." Xu Fengzhu ultimately became the governor of Zhejiang and Jiangsu provinces.

嘉兴屠康僖公，初为刑部主事，宿狱中，细询诸囚情状，得无辜者若干人，公不自以为功，密疏其事，以白堂官。后朝审，堂官摘其语，以讯诸囚，无不服者，释冤抑十馀人。

There was a man named Tu Kangxi in Jiaxing county, Zhejiang province who was once a support to the Minister of Justice, and who lived in prison at night. He was then able to interrogate the prisoners carefully and found that many of them were innocent. But Tu did not feel he had completed a good deed; he secretly reported the matter in a document to the court clerks. Later, during the autumn interrogation, the court clerks selected some key points from Tu's document and interrogated the prisoners. No one disagreed with it. The court judge thus released more than 10 prisoners who were wrongly accused and were forced to confess because they could not bear the torture.

一时辇下咸颂尚书之明。公复禀曰："辇毂之下，尚多冤民，四海之广，兆民之众，岂无枉者？宜五年差一减刑官，核实而平反之。"

For a while, people in the capital city all praised the Minister of Justice for his clear observations. Later, Tu Kangxi sent another official document to the court clerks and said: "There are so many people who have been wronged even at the feet of the emperor. In a country as big as this, with tens of thousands of people, how can there be no prisoners who have been wronged? Therefore, a commutation officer should be sent to each province every 5 years, to carefully check the facts of the prisoners' cases. If any prisoner is unjustly convicted, he should be commuted or released."

尚书为奏，允其议。时公亦差减刑之列，梦一神告之曰："汝命无子，今减刑之议，深合天心，上帝赐汝三子，皆衣紫腰金。"是夕夫人有娠，后生应埙，应坤，应埈，皆显官。

The minister reported Tu Kangxi's suggestion to the emperor, and the emperor approved it. The minister then sent a commutation officer to each province to check the prisoners' cases; Tu happened to be among the team of officers. One night, Tu dreamed of a deity telling him: "You were not destined to have a son in your life, but today your suggestion of commutation is in line with the heaven's heart, heaven will give you three sons, all of whom can be high officials, wearing purple robes with gold-inlaid belts." That night, Tu's wife became pregnant, later she gave birth to three sons: Ying Xun (1489–1529), Ying Kun (1493–?), and Ying Jun (1502–1546), all became high-ranking officials as predicted.

嘉兴包凭，字信之，其父为池阳太守，生七子，凭最少，赘平湖袁氏，与吾父往来甚厚，博学高才，累举不第，留心二氏之学。

In Jiaxing city, Zhejiang province, there was a man named Bao Ping (1486–1542), whose courtesy name was Xinzhi. His father served as the Prefect of Chiyang Residential District, Chizhou Prefecture, Anhui province, and had seven sons. Bao Ping was the youngest son who became a live-in son-in-law of the Yuan family in Pinghu county. Bao often interacted with my father, and they had a close friendship. Bao was knowledgeable and talented, but he failed the Imperial Examination every time he took it. So, he paid much attention to the studies of Daoism and Buddhism instead.

一日东游泖湖，偶至一村寺中，见观音像，淋漓露立，即解橐中十金，授主僧，令修屋宇，僧告以功大银少，不能竣事；复取松布四疋，检箧中衣七件与之，内纻褶，系新置，其仆请已之。

One day, Bao Ping toured east of Lake Mao and coincidentally arrived at a Buddhist temple in the village. He saw a Guanyin (meaning "One who perceives the sounds of the world") statue standing in the open air which was very wet from the rain. He immediately opened his bag, gave 10 taels of silver to the temple abbot, and asked him to repair the temple. The monk told him that repairing the temple was a huge project, and the money was insufficient to complete it. Bao then took four more pieces of cloth produced in Songjiang, picked seven garments of clothes from his bamboo box, and gave them to the monk, among which there was a new linen jacket, his servant asked him not to give any more.

凭曰："但得圣像无恙，吾虽裸裎何伤？"僧垂泪曰："舍银及衣布，犹非难事。只此一点心，如何易得。"后功完，拉老父同游，宿寺中。公梦伽蓝来谢曰："汝子当享世禄矣。"后子汴，孙柽芳，皆登第，作显官。

Bao Ping said: "If the Guanyin statue can be kept safe and protected from rain, does it matter if I have nothing to wear?" After hearing this, the monk shed tears and said: "It is not difficult to give away money, clothes, or cloth. But it is not easy to receive such kindness." After the temple finished repair, Bao took his father to visit it and stayed there overnight, when Bao Ping dreamed that the protector of the temple came to thank him and said: "Since you have done the good deeds, your descendants will enjoy official salaries for generations." Afterwards, his son, Bao Bian (1519–?), and grandson Bao Chengfang (1534–1596), both attained Jinshi [the highest and final degree in the Imperial Examination] and became high-ranking officials.

嘉善支立之父，为刑房吏，有囚无辜陷重辟，意哀之，欲求其生。囚语其妻曰："支公嘉意，愧无以报，明日延之下乡，汝以身事之，彼或肯用意，则我可生也。"其妻泣而听命。及至，妻自出劝酒，具告以夫意。支不听，卒为尽力平反之。

In Jiashan county, Zhejiang province, there was a man named Zhi Li (c.1472–?) whose father worked as a clerk in the execution office of the county government, where there was a prisoner who was wrongly accused and sentenced to death. Clerk Zhi felt sorry for him and wanted to plead the case to save him. The prisoner thus told his wife: "I feel ashamed of not being able to repay clerk Zhi's kindness. Tomorrow, you invite him to the countryside and marry him, he may appreciate the empathy, and I may have a chance to live." His wife cried but agreed. When clerk Zhi arrived in the countryside, the prisoner's wife came to persuade him to drink and told him about her husband's intention. Clerk Zhi did not agree to take the prisoner's wife, still he tried his best to redress the prisoner's case.

囚出狱，夫妻登门叩谢曰："公如此厚德，晚世所稀，今无子，吾有弱女，送为箕帚妾，此则礼之可通者。"支为备礼而纳之，生立，弱冠中魁，官至翰林孔目，立生高，高生禄，皆贡为学博。禄生大纶，登第。

When the prisoner was released, the couple went to kowtow and thank clerk Zhi at his house and said: "There are rare people who are as virtuous as you are in contemporary times. Since you have no son, I have a daughter whom I can send to you as your concubine, which makes logical sense." After hearing this, clerk Zhi prepared a gift and took their daughter as his concubine. Thereafter, she gave birth to a son named Zhi Li who came top in the Imperial Exam at a young age, and who became a secretary in the Hanlin Academy. Zhi Li's son was named Zhi Gao, and Zhi Gao's son was called Zhi Lu, both worked as teachers in the county school. Zhi Lu's son, Zhi Dalun (1534–1604), attained Jinshi [the highest and final degree in the Imperial Exam].

凡此十条，所行不同，同归于善而已。若复精而言之，则善有真，有假；有端，有曲；有阴，有阳；有是，有非；有偏，有正；有半，有满；有大，有小；有难，有易；皆当深辨。为善而不穷理，则自谓行持，岂知造孽，枉费苦心，无益也。

In the above ten stories, although each one did something different, they all did good deeds. If classifying good deeds more precisely, some are true, and some false; some are straight, and some twisted; some are covert, and some overt; some are correct, and some wrong; some are biased, and some justified; some are halfway, and some complete; some are big, and some small; some are difficult, and some easy. Each of them has their own principles that should be distinguished carefully. If one does good deeds without knowing the principles, they may think they do good deeds, but they commit evil, it would be a waste of effort and without benefit.

何谓真假？昔有儒生数辈，谒中峰和尚，问曰："佛氏论善恶报应，如影随形。今某人善，而子孙不兴；某人恶，而家门隆盛；佛说无稽矣。"

What is true or false? In the Yuan dynasty (1279–1368), several scholars went to see the eminent monk Zhongfeng (lit. "Middle Peak") in Mount Tianmu, they asked him: "Buddhism talks about the retribution of good and evil, just like the shadow follows the body. Wherever a person goes, the shadow follows. Why is it that someone does good deeds, yet their descendants are not prosperous; whereas someone else does evil, but their family is flourishing? There is no evidence for what Buddha said about retribution then."

中峰云："凡情未涤，正眼未开，认善为恶，指恶为善，往往有之。不憾己之是非颠倒，而反怨天之报应有差乎？"众曰："善恶何致相反？"中峰令试言。

Monk Zhongfeng replied: "Ordinary people are blinded by worldly opinions, their minds have not been cleansed, and their keen eyes have not been opened, they regard good as evil, and evil as good, this is a common phenomenon. If you have misconceptions, but you don't blame yourself for being turned upside down, how can you complain about heaven's retributions being mistaken?" Everyone asked again: "How can good and evil be turned upside down?" Monk Zhongfeng then asked them to tell all the things they considered good and evil.

一人谓："詈人殴人是恶；敬人礼人是善。"中峰云："未必然也。"一人谓："贪财妄取是恶，廉洁有守是善。"中峰云："未必然也。"众人历言其状，中峰皆谓不然。因请问。

One scholar said: "Scolding and beating others is evil; being respectful and treating others with courtesy is good." Monk Zhongfeng replied: "What you said may not be true." Another scholar said: "Being greedy for money and asking for it purposelessly is bad; being ungreedy for money and being honest and trustworthy is good." Monk Zhongfeng replied: "What you said may not be true." These scholars told all the good and bad behaviors they had seen in their lives, but monk Zhongfeng always said not all of them were true. The scholars thus asked the monk what good and evil were.

中峰告之曰："有益于人，是善；有益于己，是恶。有益于人，则殴人，詈人皆善也；有益于己，则敬人，礼人皆恶也。是故人之行善，利人者公，公则为真；

利己者私，私则为假。又根心者真，袭迹者假；又无为而为者真，有为而为者假；皆当自考。"

Monk Zhongfeng said: "Doing things that benefit others is good but benefit yourself is bad. If you do things that benefit others, even if you scold or beat them, it is still good. If you do things that only benefit yourself, then being respectful and polite to others is still bad. So, if you do good deeds that benefit the public, it is true. If you do good deeds that only benefit yourself, it is false. Thus, the deeds that come from the heart are true, and the deeds that are for formality are false. Also, if you do good deeds without asking for a reward or leaving no trace, it is true. If you do good deeds for the purpose of gaining something, it is false. You should examine all these things carefully."

何谓端曲？今人见谨愿之士，类称为善而取之；圣人则宁取狂狷。至于谨愿之士，虽一乡皆好，而必以为德之贼；是世人之善恶，分明与圣人相反。推此一端，种种取舍，无有不谬；天地鬼神之福善祸淫，皆与圣人同是非，而不与世俗同取舍。凡欲积善，决不可徇耳目，惟从心源隐微处，默默洗涤，纯是济世之心，则为端；苟有一毫媚世之心，即为曲；纯是爱人之心，则为端；有一毫愤世之心，即为曲；纯是敬人之心，则为端；有一毫玩世之心，即为曲；皆当细辨。

What is straight or twisted? Nowadays, when people see a cautious and flexible person, most people would say this is a good person to follow. However, the sages in ancient times would rather admire those who have high ambitions and who are progressive, because only these kinds of people are willing to take responsibility to do good deeds, and can teach others about progress. As for those who seem to be cautious but useless, although everyone in the village likes them, the sages consider this kind of person as thieves of virtue because they have weak personalities, follow the crowd, and have no ambition. From this point of view, ordinary people's concepts of good and evil are clearly opposite to those of sages. Extending this concept further to all other things, there is nothing ridiculous. What heaven, earth, and deities consider as good and evil, are in line with those of sages, but completely different from those of commoners. Therefore, if you want to accumulate kindness, you must not be carried away by the sounds that your ears like, or the sights that your eyes like. You must start from the hidden place where the thoughts arise and silently cleanse your heart. A heart that has full intention to help others, it is straight. A heart that has a tiny intention to flatter others, it is twisted. A heart that is full of love for others, it is straight. A heart that has a tiny resentment toward others, it is twisted. A heart that is full of respect for others, it is straight. A heart that has a tiny intention to play tricks on others, it is twisted. These things should be examined carefully.

何谓阴阳？凡为善而人知之，则为阳善；为善而人不知，则为阴德。阴德，天报之；阳善，享世名。名，亦福也。名者，造物所忌；世之享盛名而实不副者，多有奇祸；人之无过咎而横被恶名者，子孙往往骤发，阴阳之际微矣哉。

What is *yin yang*? When a person does good deeds and is known by others, it is *yang* (overt) kindness. When a person does good deeds but is unknown by others, it is *yin* (covert) virtue. Heaven knows and rewards those with *yin* virtue. A person with *yang* kindness may enjoy a worldwide reputation, and having a good reputation is also a blessing. However, heaven and earth dislike people who love fame. Just look around the world, those who enjoy great fame but have no virtue often encounter unexpected disasters; whereas those who have no fault but are wrongly accused, their descendants often have become prosperous. Therefore, the difference between *yin* virtue and *yang* kindness is subtle.

何谓是非？鲁国之法，鲁人有赎人臣妾于诸侯，皆受金于府，子贡赎人而不受金。孔子闻而恶之曰："赐失之矣。夫圣人举事，可以移风易俗，而教道可施于百姓，非独适己之行也。今鲁国富者寡而贫者众，受金则为不廉，何以相赎乎？自今以后，不复赎人于诸侯矣。"

What is right and wrong? Lu State had a law to stipulate that Lu people who were captured by other states as concubines could be redeemed, and those who paid to redeem could receive a reward from Lu State. Zigong was very rich; he redeemed people but refused to accept the reward. Confucius heard this and said angrily: "Zigong did it wrong. What a sage does, is to change the custom for the better, teach and guide people to be good, not just for self-satisfaction. Now there are few rich but more poor people in Lu State. If accepting a reward is a lack of integrity, how can those with little money redeem people? From now on, I am afraid there will be no one redeems people from other states then."

子路拯人于溺，其人谢之以牛，子路受之。孔子喜曰："自今鲁国多拯人于溺矣。"自俗眼观之，子贡不受金为优，子路之受牛为劣；孔子则取由而黜赐焉。乃知人之为善，不论现行而论流弊；不论一时而论久远；不论一身而论天下。现行虽善，其流足以害人；则似善而实非也；现行虽不善，而其流足以济人，则非善而实是也。然此就一节论之耳。他如非义之义，非礼之礼，非信之信，非慈之慈，皆当抉择。

Zilu saved a man who fell into a deep river. The man thanked Zilu by giving him an ox. Zilu accepted it. Confucius heard this and said happily: "From now on, there will be many people in Lu State who will rescue others in deep waters." From a commoner's perspective, Zigong not accepting the reward was good, whereas Zilu accepting the ox was bad. But

Confucius praised Zilu and blamed Zigong. If you want to know whether someone has done a good deed, you should not only look at their action's immediate or temporary effect but pay attention to its long-term impact. You should not only look at the individual's gains or losses but pay attention to their action's wider influence on society. If your present good deed will harm future generations, even though it looks good, it is not good. If your present bad deed will help future generations, even though it looks bad, it is good. This is just one of the many things worth paying attention to. For example, if someone has done something righteously, but they did it wrong, it is a bad thing. If someone has treated a bad person politely, but the bad person has become even more offensive, it is inappropriate politeness. If someone takes care of trust in a small thing but misses something more important, it becomes untrustworthy. Loving others is kind, but if the love causes great trouble, it becomes unkind. All these decisions should be made critically and carefully.

何谓偏正？昔吕文懿公，初辞相位，归故里，海内仰之，如泰山北斗。有一乡人，醉而詈之，吕公不动，谓其仆曰："醉者勿与较也。"闭门谢之。逾年，其人犯死刑入狱。吕公始悔之曰："使当时稍与计较，送公家责治，可以小惩而大戒；吾当时只欲存心于厚，不谓养成其恶，以至于此。"此以善心而行恶事者也。

What is partiality? In the Ming dynasty, Imperial Chancellor Lü Wenyi (1418–1462) had just resigned from his position and returned to his hometown. As he was an honest and fair official, people all over the country admired him, like all the mountains guarding Mount Tai and all the stars surrounding the Big Dipper. There was a villager who got drunk and scolded Lü. But Lü was not angry and said to his servant: "This man is drunk, don't argue with him." Lü then shut his gate and ignored the drunkard. A year later, this drunkard committed a capital crime and was imprisoned. The former chancellor Lü said regretfully: "If I had argued with him at that time and sent him to the public for punishment, he could have received a big warning through a small penalty and would not have to be sentenced to death. I just wanted to be kind and let him go. Who would know that he has developed violent behavior to such an extent!" This is an example of having a good intention but doing a bad thing in the end.

又有以恶心而行善事者。如某家大富，值岁荒，穷民白昼抢粟于市；告之县，县不理，穷民愈肆，遂私执而困辱之，众始定；不然，几乱矣。故善者为正，恶者为偏，人皆知之；其以善心行恶事者，正中偏也；以恶心而行善事者，偏中正也；不可不知也。

There are also people who have done good things though with bad intentions. For example, in a year of famine, the poor people grabbed rice from the market in the daylight. A rich family complained to the county magistrate about this, but the magistrate refused to deal with it. The poor people became even more unscrupulous. The rich family then secretly arrested the robbers and insulted them; thereafter, they stopped robbing. Otherwise, the market would have been in chaos. Although everyone knows that good is right and evil is wrong, there are instances that people who have good intentions but done bad things, and people who have bad intentions but done good things. This truth must be known.

何谓半满？易曰："善不积，不足以成名；恶不积，不足以灭身。"书曰："商罪贯盈，如贮物于器。"勤而积之，则满；懈而不积，则不满。此一说也。

What is half good? *Yi Jing* (*Book of Changes*) says: "If one does not accumulate enough good deeds, they will not build a good reputation. If one does not accumulate enough evil, they will not destroy themself." *Shang Shu* (*Book of Documents*) also says: "The faults of the Shang dynasty [c. 1600–1046 BCE] were like a string full of coins, or a container filled with collections." If one is diligent enough to accumulate good deeds, they will eventually become successful. If one is lazy and does not accumulate, they will not be successful. This is a perception of half-full good.

昔有某氏女入寺，欲施而无财，止有钱二文，捐而与之，主席者亲为忏悔；及后入宫富贵，携数千金入寺舍之，主僧惟令其徒回向而已。

In the past, there was a girl from a certain family who went to a Buddhist temple and wanted to donate funds. However, she did not have much money, only two coins, still she gave both to the chief monk. The monk then went to the Buddha statue and prayed for her in person, asking for repentance. Later, the woman entered the Imperial Palace and became a consort. Afterwards, she donated several thousand taels of silver to the temple, but the chief monk only asked his disciples to transfer the merit for her.

因问曰："吾前施钱二文，师亲为忏悔，今施数千金，而师不回向，何也？"曰："前者物虽薄，而施心甚真，非老僧亲忏，不足报德；今物虽厚，而施心不若前日之切，令人代忏足矣。"此千金为半，而二文为满也。

The woman asked the chief monk: "I once donated only two coins; Master personally repented for me. But now I'm donating several thousand taels of silver, Master doesn't transfer the merit for me. Why?" The chief monk answered: "Although the amount you donated in the past was small, your heart was sincerer, I personally repented for you because otherwise I would not be able to repay your kindness. Although the amount you are donating is large, your heart is not as genuine as before, it is enough to ask others to repent for you." This story tells that a donation of several thousand taels of silver is only half good, whereas a donation of two coins is considered full good, it all depends on the perception and circumstances.

钟离授丹于吕祖，点铁为金，可以济世。吕问曰："终变否？"曰："五百年后，当复本质。"吕曰："如此则害五百年后人矣，吾不愿为也。"曰："修仙要积三千功行，汝此一言，三千功行已满矣。"此又一说也。

Legend says Han Zhongli taught Lü Dongbin alchemy skill, which was to turn iron into gold by dropping elixir solution on the iron, a technique that could be used to relieve poverty. Dongbin asked Zhongli: "If the iron turns into gold, will it turn back to iron again?" Zhongli replied: "After 500 years, it will return back to its original form." Dongbin said: "Then it will harm people in 500 years, I am unwilling to do so." Zhongli said: "To cultivate immortality, one needs to accumulate 3,000 good deeds. Your words have completed your 3,000 good deeds." This story is another way of perceiving full good.

又为善而心不着善，则随所成就，皆得圆满。心着于善，虽终身勤励，止于半善而已。譬如以财济人，内不见己，外不见人，中不见所施之物，是谓三轮体空，是谓一心清净，则斗粟可以种无涯之福，一文可以消千劫之罪，倘此心未忘，虽黄金万镒，福不满也。此又一说也。

When one does a good deed, they should not think about it too much in their mind, as if they have done something extraordinary. If one can do so, anything they do will be complete and successful. If one does a good deed, and their mind keeps thinking about it, even if they do good deeds diligently throughout their life, it is only half good. For example, if one wants to donate money to help others, internally they should not see themselves as the giver, externally they should not see the other person as the receiver, midway they should not see the money being given, this is called "Threefold Wheel of Essential Emptiness," or "The Pure Mind." Then even though they only donate a bucket of rice, they will sow boundless blessings, or even though they only give a cent, they will eliminate a thousand calamities. If their mind cannot forget the good deeds they have done to others, even though they donate 200,000 taels of gold, their good fortune will not be full. This is another way of perceiving full good.

何谓大小？昔卫仲达为馆职，被摄至冥司，主者命吏呈善恶二录，比至，则恶录盈庭，其善录一轴，仅如箸而已。索秤称之，则盈庭者反轻，而如箸者反重。

What is big and small kindness? In the Song dynasty (960–1279), there was a man named Wei Zhongda, who was an official in the Hanlin Academy. Once, a ghost led his spirit to the netherworld. The chief judge of the netherworld ordered a clerk to bring up the two books of good and bad deeds that he had done in the world. When the booklets arrived, the judge saw that there were so many records of his bad deeds that spread all over the yard, whereas the scroll records of his good deeds were only as small as a chopstick. The judge then ordered a scale to weigh the booklets and found that the booklet of his bad deeds spread all over the yard was lighter, whereas the booklet of his good deeds as small as a chopstick was heavier.

仲达曰："某年未四十，安得过恶如是多乎？"曰："一念不正即是，不待犯也。"因问轴中所书何事？曰："朝廷尝兴大工，修三山石桥，君上疏谏之，此疏稿也。"

Wei Zhongda asked: "I am less than 40 years old, how could I have committed so many evils?" The chief judge replied: "If you have an incorrect thought, it is counted as one evil, you don't have to act on it." Wei thus asked what good deeds were recorded in the scroll. The chief judge said: "The emperor once wanted to establish a big project, to construct a stone bridge across the three mountainous areas. You wrote a memo to persuade the emperor not to implement it, so as not to waste money or exhaust people. Here is the draft of your memo."

仲达曰："某虽言，朝廷不从，于事无补，而能有如是之力。"曰："朝廷虽不从，君之一念，已在万民；向使听从，善力更大矣。"故志在天下国家，则善虽少而大；苟在一身，虽多亦小。

Wei Zhongda said: "Although I expressed my view, the emperor didn't listen and the construction proceeded, my words had no effect on the final decision of the project, how could my statement have such great power?" The chief judge said: "Although the emperor did not listen to your suggestion, your idea was to relieve tens of millions of people from exhausting labor. If the emperor listened to you, the power of your kindness would have been even greater." Therefore, if one is determined to do good deeds to benefit the country and the people, even if the good deeds are few, the merit is great. If one has decided to do good deeds only to benefit themselves, even if the good deeds are many, the merit is small.

何谓难易？先儒谓克己须从难克处克将去。夫子论为仁，亦曰先难。必如江西舒翁，舍二年仅得之束修，代偿官银，而全人夫妇。与邯郸张翁，舍十年所积之钱，代完赎银，而活人妻子，皆所谓难舍处能舍也。如镇江靳翁，虽年老无子，不忍以幼女为妾，而还之邻，此难忍处能忍也；故天降之福亦厚。凡有财有势者，其立德皆易，易而不为，是为自暴。贫贱作福皆难，难而能为，斯可贵耳。

What good deed is difficult to do? Confucian scholars in the past stated: "To control one's selfish desires, one must start with something that is difficult to dispose." Confucius discussed benevolence and said that one must first work on difficult areas, which is to overcome selfishness. For example, Mr. Shu in Jiangxi province worked as a tutor in a private home. He once donated two years' salary to help a poor family to pay back the money they owed the government, thus preventing a tragedy of the couple being separated. Another instance was Mr. Zhang from Handan, Hebei province, who donated his 10 years' savings to redeem a poor man's wife and children. Both Shu and Zhang were able to donate what others could not easily give. One more case was Mr. Jin from Zhenjiang, Jiangsu province. Although he was old and sonless, his poor neighbor was willing to give him their young daughter as a concubine in the hope of giving birth to a boy. But Jin could not bear to sacrifice the girl's youth and sent her back. This was something difficult to endure but he endured. Thus, great blessings were bestowed on these gentlemen by heaven. It is easy for those who are rich and powerful to make some merit. However, if it is easy to do and one refuses to do it, this is giving up on oneself. As for the poor who have no wealth or power, it is difficult for them to make a blessing. If it is difficult to do but one can do it, this is valuable.

随缘济众，其类至繁，约言其纲，大约有十：第一，与人为善；第二，爱敬存心；第三，成人之美；第四，劝人为善；第五，救人危急；第六，兴建大利；第七，舍财作福；第八，护持正法；第九，敬重尊长；第十，爱惜物命。

Whenever we have an opportunity, we do our best to help others in the world. There are many ways to help people, which may be summed up in ten principles: First, be kind to others. Second, love and respect others. Third, help people achieve their dreams. Fourth, persuade people to do good. Fifth, save people in critical situations. Sixth, construct big and beneficial projects. Seventh, give up property to make merit. Eighth, protect and uphold righteous principles. Ninth, respect seniors and elders. Tenth, cherish the life of all things.

何谓与人为善？昔舜在雷泽，见渔者皆取深潭厚泽，而老弱则渔于急流浅滩之中，恻然哀之，往而渔焉；见争者皆匿其过而不谈，见有让者，则揄扬而取法之。期年，皆以深潭厚泽相让矣。夫以舜之明哲，岂不能出一言教众人哉？乃不以言教而以身转之，此良工苦心也。

What does it mean to be kind to others? Before Shun became King in the Yu dynasty (c.2200–2100 BCE), he saw that young and strong fishermen all fished in the depths under Lake Leize where there were more fish; while old and weak fishermen all fished in shallow water where there were strong currents and fewer fish. Shun felt pity for the old fishermen and went fishing himself. When he saw those who liked to contest, he covered up their mistakes without telling others. When he saw those who liked to concede, he went around to praise them and set good examples for others to follow. A year later, every fisherman yielded their place in deep water to others. So, how could a sage like Shun not be able to say a few wise words to educate others? Shun did not teach people through words but acted in the scene to set good examples for others to follow to change their selfish behavior. Shun's effort was well-intentioned and painstaking.

吾辈处末世，勿以己之长而盖人；勿以己之善而形人；勿以己之多能而困人。收敛才智，若无若虚；见人过失，且涵容而掩覆之。一则令其可改，一则令其有所顾忌而不敢纵，见人有微长可取，小善可录，翻然舍己而从之；且为艳称而广述之。凡日用间，发一言，行一事，全不为自己起念，全是为物立则；此大人天下为公之度也。

Our generation was born and living in turbulent times. Do not use your strengths to overshadow others if they are not as good as you are. Do not compare your goodness with others if they have done bad things. Do not use your versatility to embarrass others if they are not as capable as you are. Restrain yourself even if you are talented and intelligent, pretend that these qualities are nothing but emptiness. When you see someone making a mistake, try to cover it up. On the one hand, it can give them a chance to correct it timely; on the other hand, they may have some scruples and dare not act recklessly. When you see someone who has some small advantages that you can learn from, or a small kindness that you can remember, put aside your judgement, learn from them, praise them, and spread good words about them. In daily life, if one's words or deeds are not to initiate any selfish desire but to set rules for others, this is a great person who has the capacity to regard everything in the world for the public rather than the private.

何谓爱敬存心？君子与小人，就形迹观，常易相混，惟一点存心处，则善恶悬绝，判然如黑白之相反。故曰：君子所以异于人者，以其存心也。君子所存之心，只是爱人敬人之心。盖人有亲疏贵贱，有智愚贤不肖；万品不齐，皆吾同胞，皆吾一体，孰非当敬爱者？爱敬众人，即是爱敬圣贤；能通众人之志，即是通圣贤之志。何者？圣贤之志，本欲斯世斯人，各得其所。吾合爱合敬，而安一世之人，即是为圣贤而安之也。

What is love and respect? Judging from appearance, one may find it difficult to distinguish between the virtuous and the villainous. The only difference is in their intentions, the virtuous have good goals whereas the villainous have evil aims, which set them far apart, like black and white, the two opposite colors. Thus, Mengzi said: "The difference between a virtuous person and an ordinary person is in their intentions." A virtuous heart is only to love and respect others. There may be many different types of people who can be close, distant, noble, humble, wise, unwise, honorable, and dishonorable; but they are all our compatriots, and we are all one, whom should we not love and respect? To love and respect everyone is to love and respect sages. To know everyone's aspirations is to know sages' aspirations. Why? Sages hope that everyone in the world can live a happy and peaceful life. Thus, if we love and respect everyone so that people in the world can be safe and satisfied, that is to protect everyone on behalf of sages.

何谓成人之美？玉之在石，抵掷则瓦砾，追琢则圭璋；故凡见人行一善事，或其人志可取而资可进，皆须诱掖而成就之。或为之奖借，或为之维持；或为白其诬而分其谤；务使成立而后已。

How can you help others achieve their dreams? For example, if someone throws away a stone with jade inside, it will be just like a piece of worthless gravel. If one carves and polishes the stone properly, it will become a precious treasure. So, if you see someone doing a good deed, or someone is determined to do a good deed and is capable to complete it, you should guide them and help them achieve their aims; or you should praise them and support them. If they are wrongly accused, you should defend them and share their slander, so that they can stand up to social pressure. Only then, you will have done your best.

大抵人各恶其非类，乡人之善者少，不善者多。善人在俗，亦难自立。且豪杰铮铮，不甚修形迹，多易指摘；故善事常易败，而善人常得谤；惟仁人长者，匡直而辅翼之，其功德最宏。

Generally, people dislike those who are different from themselves. There are more villagers who are unkind than those who are kind. Thus, kind people are often bullied and are difficult to establish themselves. Moreover, the exceptional normally have upright and unyielding personalities who do not pay attention to their appearance and are often criticized by the laity. Therefore, good people often fail to complete their good deeds and are often slandered. Only benevolent elders can correct and teach bad people, protect and help good people to establish themselves, whose merits are really the greatest.

何谓劝人为善？生为人类，孰无良心？世路役役，最易没溺。凡与人相处，当方便提撕，开其迷惑。譬犹长夜大梦，而令之一觉；譬犹久陷烦恼，而拔之清凉，为惠最溥。韩愈云："一时劝人以口，百世劝人以书。"较之与人为善，虽有形迹，然对证发药，时有奇效，不可废也；失言失人，当反吾智。

How can we persuade others to do good? We were born as human beings in this world, who has no conscience? Because people have relentless desires for fame and fortune, they can fall easily. Therefore, when we deal with others, we should remind them at times to clear up their misconceptions. For example, if we see someone having a nightmare during a long night, we should wake them up immediately. Or, if we see someone getting stuck in a situation for a long time, we should help them calm their mind. Treating others with such kindness will accumulate the biggest merits. Confucian scholar Han Yu (768–824) said: "Persuading others with a speech can only last for a while, persuading others with books can last for generations." Compared with the previous discussion on being kind to others, it now offers formal suggestions, this kind of prescribing the right medicine often has wonderful effects, which must not be abandoned. When we persuade others to do good, we must do this properly according to their personalities and possible reactions. If we mislead others, it may have adverse effects. We must practice self-reflection carefully.

何谓救人危急？患难颠沛，人所时有。偶一遇之，当如痌瘝之在身，速为解救。或以一言伸其屈抑；或以多方济其颠连。崔子曰："惠不在大，赴人之急可也。"盖仁人之言哉。

How can we save others in a critical situation? Trouble and adversity occasionally occur in people's lives. If we happen to see someone in distress, we should treat their pain as ours and rescue them as soon as possible. If they have been wronged or oppressed, either defend them with words, or relieve their hardship with other methods. Neo-Confucian scholar Cui Xian (1478–1541) said: "It does not matter how big our favor is, as long as we help others in their crisis." This advice is truly from a benevolent sage.

何谓兴建大利？小而一乡之内，大而一邑之中，凡有利益，最宜兴建；或开渠导水，或筑堤防患；或修桥梁，以便行旅；或施茶饭，以济饥渴；随缘劝导，协力兴修，勿避嫌疑，勿辞劳怨。

What is constructing big and beneficial projects? Anything that will benefit the public, either small projects in a town, or big projects in a county, should be constructed. For example, dig waterways to irrigate farmland, build embankments to prevent floods, construct bridges to facilitate travel, and provide food and tea to hungry and thirsty people. Whenever we encounter an opportunity, we persuade others to work together and contribute to construction. Do not refrain ourselves from doing good deeds just to avoid doubt by others. Do not fear hard work or possible resentment by others.

何谓舍财作福？释门万行，以布施为先。所谓布施者，只是舍之一字耳。达者内舍六根，外舍六尘，一切所有，无不舍者。苟非能然，先从财上布施。世人以衣食为命，故财为最重。吾从而舍之，内以破吾之悭，外以济人之急；始而勉强，终则泰然，最可以荡涤私情，祛除执吝。

What is giving up property to make merit? According to Buddhism, there are thousands of good deeds, but giving is the first thing to do. For the givers, internally it is to be able to cede one's eyes, ears, nose, tongue, body, and thoughts; and externally stop sensing color, sound, smell, taste, touch, and object. Nothing that a person has cannot be given up. If one cannot give up anything, start with money first. Ordinary people regard food and clothing as vital as life, so they consider money as the most important thing in life. If one can give money away to people who need it, internally they can stop being miserly; externally they can help others in times of emergency. However, one may feel a little reluctant to do it at first, once they get used to letting it go, their heart will eventually feel at ease. This is the easiest way to stop being selfish, or stop being stingy with money.

何谓护持正法？法者，万世生灵之眼目也。不有正法，何以参赞天地？何以裁成万物？何以脱尘离缚？何以经世出世？故凡见圣贤庙貌，经书典籍，皆当敬重而修饬之。至于举扬正法，上报佛恩，尤当勉励。

What is protecting and upholding righteous principles? Natural laws have been the vision of all living things for thousands of years. If there are no such natural laws, how can we participate in creating things with heaven and earth? How can all things be as fitting as tailoring clothes? How can we eliminate all confusions and constraints? How can we manage the world and escape from the process of death and rebirth? Thus, whenever we see sages' temples, images, and classics, we should respect these and repair the damaged parts. As for upholding righteous principles, we should repay the kindness of Buddha and practice these principles in all our affairs.

何谓敬重尊长？家之父兄，国之君长，与凡年高，德高，位高，识高者，皆当加意奉事。在家而奉侍父母，使深爱婉容，柔声下气，习以成性，便是和气格天之本。出而事君，行一事，毋谓君不知而自恣也。刑一人，毋谓君不知而作威也。事君如天，古人格论，此等处最关阴德。试看忠孝之家，子孙未有不绵远而昌盛者，切须慎之。

What is respecting seniors and elders? One should respect their father and brothers at home, the monarch and ministers in the country, and anyone who is older, or has a higher moral character, a higher position, or more knowledge. To serve parents, one must have a deep love for them, a gentle appearance, a calm voice, and turn this habit into a natural disposition. This is the basis of harmony moving heaven's heart. To serve the monarch in office, one must do everything according to the laws of the country, do not do anything at will just because the monarch does not know. When dealing with someone who committed a crime, one must interrogate carefully, enforce the law fairly, and not be arrogant or unjust because the monarch does not know. When serving the monarch, one must show respect as if serving heaven, which is the norm set by the ancients. This kind of conduct has the closest connection with hidden virtues. Look at a loyal and filial family, their descendants all have a good future, so one must do everything prudently.

何谓爱惜物命？凡人之所以为人者，惟此恻隐之心而已；求仁者求此，积德者积此。周礼，"孟春之月，牺牲毋用牝。"孟子谓君子远庖厨，所以全吾恻隐之心也。故前辈有四不食之戒，谓闻杀不食，见杀不食，自养者不食，专为我杀者不食。学者未能断肉，且当从此戒之。

What is cherishing the life of all things? People can be regarded as human beings because we have compassion. To seek benevolence is to seek compassion, and to accumulate virtue is to accumulate compassion. *The Rites of Zhou* says: "The first lunar month of every year is when animals are most likely to become pregnant. At this time, female animals should not be used for sacrifice to prevent the embryos from being killed." Mengzi also said the virtuous should stay away from bloody killing. Thus, we should all preserve our compassion. So, the elder generations had four taboos against eating meat. If they heard an animal being killed, they would not eat it. If they saw the animal being killed, they would not eat it. If they raised the animal themselves, they would not eat it. If the animal was killed specially for them, they would not eat it. For the younger generations who cannot stop eating meat, they should follow the methods of the elderly and quit eating meat afterwards.

渐渐增进，慈心愈长，不特杀生当戒，蠢动含灵，皆为物命。求丝煮茧，锄地杀虫，念衣食之由来，皆杀彼以自活。故暴殄之孽，当与杀生等。至于手所误伤，足所误践者，不知其几，皆当委曲防之。古诗云："爱鼠常留饭，怜蛾不点灯。"何其仁也！

Even if one cannot stop eating meat immediately, they should reduce meat consumption while their compassion increases gradually. Not only should one refrain from killing but also stop harming the lives of those very small and frivolous beings, if they are alive. For example, boiling silkworm cocoons in water to make clothes will kill many silkworms, and hoeing ground for farming will kill many insects. Think about where food and clothes come from, all from killing others to serve ourselves. Therefore, the sin of wasting food and clothes is equal to that of killing. One may not know exactly how many lives they have accidentally injured or mistakenly stepped on, but people should prevent such things from happening again. Su Shi (1037–1101) wrote these two lines in a poem: "If you love mice, always leave some food for them; if you pity moths, do not lit a lamp." How benevolent these words are!

善行无穷，不能殚述；由此十事而推广之，则万德可备矣。

There are endless good deeds that cannot be all described here. If the ten principles are spread and promoted, countless virtues can be accumulated.

了凡四训·第四章·谦德之效
Liaofan's Four Lessons
Lesson 4: Effects of Modesty and Virtue

易曰："天道亏盈而益谦；地道变盈而流谦；鬼神害盈而福谦；人道恶盈而好谦。"是故谦之一卦，六爻皆吉。

The Book of Changes' Qian hexagram says: "The principles of heaven are that whoever is complacent will lose, and whoever is humble will gain. The principles of earth are that whoever is complacent will be changed, and whoever is humble will be fulfilled. The principles of divine spirits are that whoever is complacent will be harmed, and whoever is humble will be blessed. The principles of humans are that whoever is complacent will be disliked, and whoever is humble will be liked." Among the *Book of* Changes' 64 hexagrams, only the Qian hexagram has an auspicious meaning in every line, the rest all have mixed good and bad omens.

书曰："满招损，谦受益。" 予屡同诸公应试，每见寒士将达，必有一段谦光可掬。

The Book of Documents also says: "Complacency will bring harm, whereas humility will bring benefit." I went to take the exam with many people several times. Every time I saw poor scholars who were about to pass the exam and became prosperous, their faces would look humble and serene, as if it could be held in hands.

辛未（公元1571年）计偕，我嘉善同袍凡十人，惟丁敬宇宾，年最少，极其谦虚。予告费锦坡曰："此兄今年必第。"费曰："何以见之？"

In the year of Xinwei (1571), I went to take the exam with ten fellows from Jiashan county, Zhejiang province, there was a man named Ding Jingyu (1543–c.1633) who was the youngest and very humble. I told Fei Jinpo who was also taking the exam: "This man will surely pass the exam this year." Fei asked me: "How can you tell?"

予曰："惟谦受福。兄看十人中，有恂恂款款，不敢先人，如敬宇者乎？有恭敬顺承，小心谦畏，如敬宇者乎？有受侮不答，闻谤不辩，如敬宇者乎？人能如此，即天地鬼神，犹将佑之，岂有不发者？"及开榜，丁果中式。

I said: "Only humble people are given blessings. Brother, look at the ten of us, is there anyone who is honest and kind, and dare not get ahead of others in everything, like Jingyu? Is there anyone who is respectful and humble, and tries to accept everything, like Jingyu? Is there anyone who refuses to answer when someone insults them, or refuses to argue when someone slanders them, like Jingyu? If one can be like this, even heaven, earth, and divine spirit will protect them. Is there any reason for them not to pass the exam?" When the results were released, Ding Jingyu indeed passed the exam.

丁丑（公元1577年）在京，与冯开之同处，见其虚己敛容，大变其幼年之习。李霁岩直谅益友，时面攻其非，但见其平怀顺受，未尝有一言相报。予告之曰："福有福始，祸有祸先，此心果谦，天必相之，兄今年决第矣。"已而果然。

In the year of Dingchou (1577), I was in the capital city living with Feng Kaizhi (1548–c.1595). I saw that he was always humble with a gentle face and had greatly changed his childhood habits. Feng had an upright and honest friend named Li Jiyan, who was straightforward and sometimes criticized Feng's faults in person. But I saw that Feng had always calmly accepted Li's critiques without rebuttal. I told Feng: "Good fortune has roots, and misfortune has signs. As your heart is so humble, heaven must help you, brother, you will get the first place this year." Feng Kaizhi passed the exam.

赵裕峰，光远，山东冠县人，童年举于乡，久不第。其父为嘉善三尹，随之任。慕钱明吾，而执文见之，明吾悉抹其文，赵不惟不怒，且心服而速改焉。明年，遂登第。

Zhao Yufeng, style-named Guangyuan, was a native of Guan county, Shandong province. When he was young, he passed the provincial exam but later failed the national exam many times. His father was the Chief Secretary of Jiashan county, and Yufeng helped his father in the office. Zhao Yufeng admired Qian Mingwu's knowledge, so he went to see him with his own article. Mingwu crossed all his writing. Not only did Zhao remain calm, but he was also convinced and quickly corrected all the flaws in the article. In the following year, Zhao Yufeng passed the national exam.

壬辰岁（公元1592年），予入觐，晤夏建所，见其人气虚意下，谦光逼人，归而告友人曰："凡天将发斯人也，未发其福，先发其慧；此慧一发，则浮者自实，肆者自敛；建所温良若此，天启之矣。"及开榜，果中式。

In the year of Renchen (1592), I went to the capital city to see the emperor, and met a scholar named Xia Jiansuo. I saw that he had a mild temperament, and that his humble brilliance seemed to radiate positivity to others. After returning home, I told my friends: "Whenever heaven wants to make someone prosperous, it must first grant them wisdom.

Once wisdom is granted, a frivolous person will become honest, and an unbridled person will become restrained. As Jiansuo is so gentle and kind, heaven has granted him wisdom, and his blessings will come." When the results were released, Xia Jiansuo passed the exam.

江阴张畏岩，积学工文，有声艺林。甲午（公元 1594 年），南京乡试，寓一寺中，揭晓无名，大骂试官，以为眯目。时有一道者，在傍微笑，张遽移怒道者。道者曰："相公文必不佳。"张怒曰："汝不见我文，乌知不佳？"道者曰："闻作文，贵心气和平，今听公骂詈，不平甚矣，文安得工？"

Zhang Weiyan was a native of Jiangyin county, Jiangsu province. He accumulated profound knowledge, wrote good articles, and was well-known among contemporary scholars. In the year of Jiawu (1594), he went to take the Nanjing Provincial Examination and rented a room in a temple nearby. When the results were released, his name was not on the list. He scolded the examiner for not being able to see the good in his article. While a Daoist sage was by the side smiling, Zhang redirected his anger toward the Daoist sage. The Daoist said: "Your article must not be good." Zhang responded angrily: "You haven't read my article, how do you know it isn't good?" The Daoist said: "I often hear people say that when writing, one must have a gentle and quiet spirit. Now that I hear you yelling at the examiner, you are so uncalm, how can your article be good?"

张不觉屈服，因就而请教焉。道者曰："中全要命；命不该中，文虽工，无益也。须自己做个转变。"张曰："既是命，如何转变？"道者曰："造命者天，立命者我；力行善事，广积阴德，何福不可求哉？"

Zhang Weiyan unconsciously surrendered after hearing the Daoist sage's words, so he asked for his advice. The Daoist said: "Passing the exam all depends on one's fate. If your fate is not to succeed in it, even if your article is good, it will not help you pass the exam. You must change your destiny yourself." Zhang said: "Since it is fate, how can I change it?" The Daoist said: "The power to create destiny lies in heaven, but the power to establish destiny lies in ourselves. If you try your best to do good, and extensively accumulate hidden virtues, what blessings cannot be obtained?"

张曰："我贫士，何能为？"道者曰："善事阴功，皆由心造，常存此心，功德无量，且如谦虚一节，并不费钱，你如何不自反而骂试官乎？"张由此折节自持，善日加修，德日加厚。

Zhang Weiyan said: "I am a poor scholar, what good deeds can I do?" The Daoist sage replied: "Doing good deeds and accumulating hidden virtues are all from the heart. If you keep this in your heart, your good deeds and hidden virtues will be boundless. Like being modest, you don't have to spend money on it, why don't you reflect on yourself instead of scolding the examiner for being unfair?" After hearing the Daoist sage's words, Zhang suppressed his proud ambition and paid great attention to restraining himself. He worked hard every day to cultivate goodness and accumulate virtues.

丁酉（公元 1597 年），梦至一高房，得试录一册，中多缺行。问旁人，曰："此今科试录。"问："何多缺名？"曰："科第阴间三年一考较，须积德无咎者，方有名。如前所缺，皆系旧该中式，因新有薄行而去之者也。"后指一行云："汝三年来，持身颇慎，或当补此，幸自爱。"是科果中一百五名。

In the year of Dingyou (1597), Zhang Weiyan dreamed of entering a very tall building and saw a roster of exam admissions with many missing names in the lines. He asked the person nearby: "What is this?" The person replied: "This is the list of people who passed this year's Imperial Exam." Zhang asked again: "Why are there so many missing names in the list?" The person replied again: "The netherworld will test triennially those who take the exam. The candidates must have accumulated enough good deeds without fault, so that their names will remain in the book. The vacancies at the front are those who should have passed the exam, but due to their recent faults, their names have been removed." Later, the person pointed at another line and said: "In the past 3 years, you have carefully restrained yourself. Maybe it's time to fill the gap. I hope you cherish yourself." Zhang Weiyan indeed passed the exam in 105th place.

由此观之，举头三尺，决有神明；趋吉避凶，断然由我。须使我存心制行，毫不得罪于天地鬼神，而虚心屈己，使天地鬼神，时时怜我，方有受福之基。彼气盈者，必非远器，纵发亦无受用。稍有识见之士，必不忍自狭其量，而自拒其福也，况谦则受教有地，而取善无穷，尤修业者所必不可少者也。

Therefore, it seems that there must be divine spirit three feet above our heads observing our behavior. As such, things that are auspicious and beneficial to others should be done promptly, and things that are dangerous and harmful to others should be avoided. These decisions can be made by us. If we have good intentions, restrain unwholesome behavior, do not offend heaven, earth, or divine spirit in the slightest, be humble and adaptable without being arrogant, heaven, earth, and divine spirit will always have mercy on us, only then we will have the basis of receiving blessings. Those who are full of arrogance are not visionaries, even if they can become prosperous, they will not enjoy blessings for a long time. A person with some knowledge will not narrow their mind to refuse the blessings they can receive. Moreover, being modest will allow one to have the capacity to receive further education, so that their learned kindness from others will be endless, especially for those who pursue moral cultivation, modesty is essential.

古语云："有志于功名者，必得功名；有志于富贵者，必得富贵。"人之有志，如树之有根，立定此志，须念念谦虚，尘尘方便，自然感动天地，而造福由我。今之求登科第者，初未尝有真志，不过一时意兴耳；兴到则求，兴阑则止。

There is an old saying from the ancients: "Those who seek fame will become famous, and those who seek wealth will become wealthy." A person with lofty goals is like a tree with roots. Once we have set an ambitious goal, we must be modest in every way. Even if we encounter some barriers as small as dust, we must make it convenient for others. If we can do so, we will certainly move heaven and earth, and blessings will be created by us. Those who seek fame today may not be pursuing it sincerely from the beginning, it may just be their temporary interest. When the interest comes, they seek it, and when the interest subsides, they stop it.

孟子曰："王之好乐甚，齐其庶几乎？"予于科名亦然。

Mengzi said to King Xuan of Qi (c.350–301 BCE): "Your Majesty love music greatly. If your interest in music extends from a mere personal pursuit of happiness to making all the people happy, will the State of Qi not be prosperous?" I think the same is true for seeking fame. If we can manifest our desires for fame into accumulating virtues and doing good deeds, and we do so with all our hearts, then we make our own choices and we determine our own destinies.

www.ingramcontent.com/pod-product-compliance
Lightning Source LLC
Chambersburg PA
CBHW081404070526
44583CB00020B/2677